THE VEGETARIAN COOKBOOK

THE VEGETARIAN COOKBOOK

JUDY RIDGWAY

WARD LOCK LIMITED · LONDON

First published in Great Britain in 1985
by Ward Lock Limited, 82 Gower Street,
London WC1E 6EQ.

Text filmset in Monotype Goudy Oldstyle
by Hourds Typographica.

Printed and bound in Italy by Sagdos SpA.

British Library Cataloguing in Publication Data

Ridgway, Judy
   The vegetarian cookbook.
   1. Vegetarian cookery
   I. Title
   641.5'636   TX837

   ISBN 0-7063-6379-5

CONTENTS

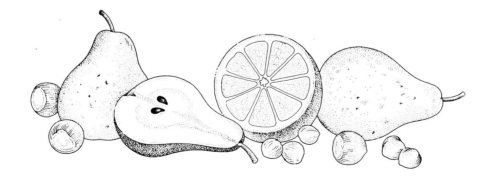

Acknowledgements

Cover photograph by Eric Carter

Photography on pages 17, 20, 25, 37, 41, 61, 65, 73 and 77
by Peter Myers
Home Economist   Clare Gordon-Smith
Stylist   Alison Williams

Photography on pages 29, 49 and 53
by Edmund Goldspink

Line drawings   Paul Saunders

The author and publisher would like to thank the
following companies for sponsoring photographs:

Knorr Stock Cubes (page 25); Mazola Corn Oil (page 41);
Mushroom Growers Association (page 20);
US Rice Council and California Raisin Advisory Board
(page 61) **and** Whitworths Ltd (pages 37 and 77)

Notes

It is important to follow the metric, imperial *or* American measures when using the recipes in this book. Do not use a combination of measures.

American terminology within recipes is indicated by the use of brackets in both the list of ingredients and in the methods.

American measures which follow metric and imperial measures within the recipe methods are preceded by the term 'US'.

Recipes use dried herbs unless otherwise indicated. If using fresh herbs, double the given quantity.

All recipes serve four people.

INTRODUCTION

There is no doubt that vegetarian eating is increasing greatly. The reasons for this are many and varied, including a growing interest in nutrition generally.

Experts are advocating a reduction in the amount of fat eaten in the diet together with an increase in the amount of fibre consumed. Fortunately, the absence of meat will substantially reduce fat intake while the use of whole grain products and plenty of fruit and vegetables – the main sources of fibre – constitute the basis of the vegetarian diet.

What is a Vegetarian?

The majority of vegetarians are known as *lacto-vegetarians*; ie they shun the flesh of animals which have been slaughtered, but will eat dairy products such as butter, cheese and eggs. There are, however, other vegetarians who avoid any kind of food which does not come from plants. These people are known as *vegans*.

This book is aimed at lacto-vegetarians, though some dishes are included which would be suitable for vegans. In other recipes, soya milk or tofu could be substituted for the dairy milk, yoghurt or soft cheese.

The recipes in this book are suitable both for everyday and for entertaining, and, just as important, will appeal both to the vegetarian and non-vegetarian alike.

Judy Ridgway

Planning a Balanced Vegetarian Diet

Planning your eating so that you have a balanced diet means selecting the right mixture of foods to maintain good health, ie foods containing some or all the essential nutrients (see below). Additionally, and of equal importance, it also means selecting foods that taste and look attractive. After all there is no point in producing an extremely healthy meal if it looks unattractive and you and your family simply do not want to eat it.

Nutritional Balance

On the nutritional front, there are a number of essential nutrients that the body must have to function properly. These are proteins, carbohydrates, fats, vitamins and minerals. Many of them are found in different sorts of food and, in theory, it does not matter which kind of food you get them from, provided that you do get them.

When it comes to protein, however, this is a bit of a simplification. The quality of the protein is important since not all proteins are the same. If they were, there would be no problem for most dairy produce, and many plants have an excellent showing on the quantity scale.

All proteins are made up of a combination of the same 22 amino acids, some of which are produced naturally in the body. But eight of these are not, and for the building of new body proteins to continue, these eight essential amino acids must be provided from proteins eaten in the daily diet. Additionally, they need to be present simultaneously and in the right proportions, otherwise protein synthesis will fall to a very low level.

All the essential amino acids are present in most foods, but unfortunately they do not necessarily occur in the ideal proportions for the body to use. There are usually one or more amino acids present in disproportionately small quantities. This means that if half the ideal proportions of one of the essential amino acids is missing from a protein, then the body can only use half the total quantity of all the other essential amino acids present; the rest is wasted or used to supply energy. It also means that twice the amount of that protein would need to be eaten to fulfil daily requirements. The most deficient amino acid is called the limiting amino acid.

The highest quality proteins would be those in which there was no limiting amino acid and all the protein was usable by the body. The protein in eggs comes very near to this ideal. Animal proteins occupy the highest rungs on the usability scale, and for this reason they used to be classed as first class proteins. Meat is, however, not at the top; milk, cheese and fish are all higher up the scale.

Some vegetable proteins approach the level of meat, and these include soya beans and whole rice. The rest of the nuts and pulses are in lower usability ranges, and this, of course, means that it would be necessary to eat rather a lot of them to cover daily requirements because of the limiting amino acids waste. This is an important consideration in a vegan diet.

For lacto-vegetarians the situation is very much easier. Dairy produce is high on the usability scale, and some of them – dried skimmed milk and Parmesan cheese for example – are also high on the percentage quantity scale. Contrary to popular belief, vegetarians do not miss out in the protein stakes.

COMPLEMENTARY PROTEINS

It would, however, be a pity to dismiss plant proteins out

of hand – they are cheap and plentiful and add great variety to the diet. The trick is to eat proteins that have mutually complementary amino acid patterns, ie one protein that is low in one particular amino acid is matched with a protein that is rich in the same amino acid. In this way the protein value of the meal is increased so that the whole is greater than the sum of the parts. This is because the matching of amino acids means that more of each protein is available for use by the body. Such protein mixes do not result in a perfect protein but they can increase the protein quantity by as much as 50% above the average of the items eaten separately.

Many people unconsciously take advantage of this complementary effect. Bread and cheese complement each other very well, for example. Baked beans on toast is another example; here the combination of wheat and beans can increase the amount of usable protein by up to 33%.

THE VEGETARIAN DIET

Perhaps the easiest way to plan a balanced vegetarian diet is to divide food into categories according to its major attributes and then to choose larger or smaller amounts from each group for each meal. Below are five groups of food selected in just this way.

1) *Bread, cereals, rice, pasta and potatoes*: This group supplies carbohydrates for energy along with various vitamins and minerals such as B group vitamins, vitamin E, calcium and iron. The cereals also provide important amounts of protein and dietary fibre.

2) *Pulses, nuts and seeds*: This group also supplies protein, and when eaten with protein from group 1) can yield an even greater amount of usable protein (see complementary proteins above).

3) *Vegetables and fruit*: This group supplies vitamins, particularly Vitamin C, and plenty of minerals and dietary fibre.

4) *Milk, eggs and cheese*: This group supplies protein, calcium and Vitamins A and D. It may also, however, be supplying fat and cholesterol so that it is important, where possible, to choose skimmed milk and low fat cheeses.

5) *Butter, margarine and cooking oil*: This group supplies fats for longer term energy plus Vitamins A and D, and is the section to cut down on. Remember to check on the ingredients list of items such as crisps (potato chips), chocolate, mayonnaise and salad dressings since they may contain 'hidden' fat.

It is obvious from the above categories that protein-rich foods may fall into three of these categories so that as a vegetarian your daily protein requirement may not come from one large important item at the main meal of the day. In fact, it is much more likely that it will come from the sum total of all the protein-containing foods eaten during the day.

It is, therefore, easy to enhance the protein value of a particular dish either by adding extra protein-rich ingredients or by making use of the complementary protein theory.

The three most effective combinations of protein foods are milk products and grains, pulses and grains, and pulses and seeds. Set out below are some good examples of these combinations and some hints on putting them into practice.

Milk products and grains

Cereals with milk: muesli (granola)
Bread and cheese: sandwiches, Welsh Rarebit
Cheese and rice: rissoles and patties
Milk, cheese and cornmeal: polenta
Milk and wheatflour: sauces
Cheese and pasta: baked casseroles

Try adding skimmed milk or low-fat cheese or yoghurt to potato dishes. The greater the amount of the milk product, the better the overall protein value.

Use non-fat dried milk with grains and pulses. Do not bother to dilute it – just add it in its dry state.

Pulses and grains

Beans and wheatflour or bread: baked beans on toast
Peas and beans with rice: risotto
Beans and corn: vegetable casseroles

When using pulses and rice, the best combination from a complementary protein point of view is about 3:1 grains to pulses. If the recipe calls for a higher ratio of beans, add some milk products or seeds.

Use soya flour in cakes and pastries to give a good short texture as well as to increase the protein content. Soya flour can also be added to bread and pancakes. Use to replace flour on a 7:1 ratio.

Add soya flour to pâtés, terrines and rissoles.

Pulses and seeds

Chick-peas and sesamé seeds: Houmous
Beans and nuts: terrines and pâtés
Beans and sunflower seeds: vegetable stuffings

All bean dishes are enhanced protein-wise by the addition of a milk product. Serve butter beans (dried lima or white kidney beans) in white sauce or red beans with cottage cheese and herbs.

Add nuts and seeds to salads and to vegetable dishes.

Add protein to desserts by including soya flour or ground nuts in crunchy toppings and in pastry.

Note Remember that peanuts are legumes or pulses *not* nuts.

Presenting Individual Meals

As well as fulfilling nutritional and health requirements, a meal should be an enjoyable pastime and there are a number of simple factors which can really make a difference to the appeal and taste of a meal.

The first of these is the choice of flavourings to be used. This is a particularly important consideration for vegetarian food which too often tends to be insipid or bland. Of course, nuts, pulses and cereals do have a flavour of their own but these can often be greatly enhanced by the careful choice of flavourings. It is, therefore, important to experiment with flavourings. But do not go mad on the latest discovery and use it in every dish. The same herb or spice in the main dish, sauce and starter would become extremely monotonous.

Texture, too, is important. It is not good dietetically, nor does it make an interesting meal, if there is more than one dish prepared and finished in the same way. Several dishes made with pastry or deep-fried would be boring as well as unhealthy. So it is best to vary the textures by serving crunchy vegetables with light soufflés and smooth dishes, a smooth sauce with pastry dishes, and rice or potatoes with casseroles.

The look of the food can also set the taste-buds working. Mix colours as well as textures, and avoid food that is all white or all brown. Arrange the food attractively on serving dishes or individual plates, and use garnishes to improve its appearance. Parsley, crumbled egg yolk, tomatoes, watercress and roasted nuts are all effective, and you can easily experiment with other things.

On the whole, we are used to three course meals with a central course consisting of a main dish with vegetables. The emphasis can, however, shift a little with vegetarian meals. Sometimes the dishes will all have equal weight. But do make sure that there are not too many rich or fatty dishes in the same meal. This can be both over-facing and bad for the digestion.

One final point concerns the balance of raw and cooked foods. To some extent, this will depend on your own inclinations and convictions. It is, nonetheless, a fact that fresh raw food often contains more of its original nutrients. This is because some vitamins are destroyed by heat and others are leached out into the cooking liquor which is often thrown away.

Some experts suggest that a raw food dish should be used to start every meal, and this is a convenient method of making sure that you have a regular intake of raw foods. Other people like to eat at least one raw food or salad meal each day. But whatever style of eating you choose, do make sure that you do not overcook your food – particularly vegetables, and that you do not leave chopped or grated raw food exposed to the air – both are sure ways of losing much of their goodness.

BASIC INGREDIENTS AND THEIR PREPARATION

The vast majority of ingredients used in the recipes in this book are to be found in large supermarkets, and most of it is everyday produce easily available. A few items such as flaked millet, buckwheat, gelozone and agar-agar will, however, require a visit to a specialist grocer or to the local health food store. And it is probably sensible to stock up on canned artichoke hearts, water chestnuts or flageolet beans when you happen to see them.

Herbs and spices are particularly important in vegetarian cooking, so stock up and experiment with as wide a range as you can find. If you have a garden, grow as wide a variety as you can. Use them fresh in summer, and dry them for the winter months, but remember that you will need to use rather more of the fresh herbs than the dried ones.

Basic Equipment

There is a common misconception that vegetarian cookery takes ages to prepare—all that chopping and grinding! But this is not really the case. All good cooking does, however, take some time to prepare, so a careful selection of useful equipment can help to cut down preparation time.

The vegetarian cook does not really need much in the way of extra equipment, though a food processor is a big help if you are keen on salads, and a pressure cooker dramatically cuts the time that beans take to cook. So plan your kitchen in the normal way, adding some of the items listed below, depending on the type of food you like to prepare and the size of your pocket.

French cook's knife—your basic tool for most dishes
Food processor
Blender-liquidizer with grinder attachment
Mouli-mill for soups and purées—this gives a coarser texture than a liquidizer
Pressure cooker
Double saucepan (boiler)
Two or three stainless steel steamers to fit inside your pans
Wire whisk for sauces

A good set of pans is a really worthwhile investment. Go for stainless steel—with a copper base if you can afford it. Alternatively, enamelled cast iron is fine although you should not use it if it chips. Many people believe that aluminium is dangerous and copper kills any vitamin C that remains during cooking. A thick base spreads the heat—this is particularly important when using a hob.

The Store Cupboard

A store cupboard is always useful and this is particularly true for the vegetarian cook. Some items require advance cooking. It is no good rushing out to buy black-eye beans, for example, the day you want to eat them since they require a long soaking period and will not be ready until the next day. Other items such as herbs and spices are in constant demand and need to be on hand.

Below (and over) is a check-list of most of the items I keep in my own store cupboard.

HERBS

Thyme, marjoram, basil, sage, summer savory, rosemary, tarragon, chives, dill weed, chervil, oregano, bay leaves, mint, parsley, fennel and dill.

SPICES

Allspice; whole and ground cumin seed, caraway seeds, dill seed; celery seed and celery salt, turmeric, cardamoms; whole and ground coriander, cloves; ground, root and stem ginger; nutmeg and mace, cinnamon, curry powder, mixed spices; black and white, Cayenne and paprika pepper, sea salt.

FLAVOURINGS AND SAUCES

Vanilla and almond essence (extract), garlic and garlic salt, tomato purée (paste), French (Dijon-style) and English mustard, yeast (vegetable) extract, cider and wine vinegar, tomato ketchup, vegetarian stock (bouillon) cubes.

NUTS, PULSES AND SEEDS

Peanuts, almonds, walnuts, cashew nuts, hazelnuts (filberts), peanut butter, sesame seeds, sunflower seeds, soya flour, lentils and a selection of dried peas and beans.

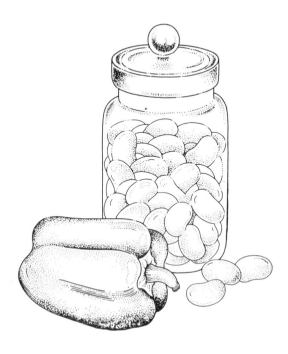

CEREALS

Wholemeal (wholewheat) flour and 81% extraction self-raising flour, fine and medium oatmeal, rolled oats, buckwheat, flaked barley, flaked millet, muesli (granola) mix, yellow cornmeal, brown rice and a selection of wholemeal (wholewheat) pasta.

PRESERVES AND SWEETENERS

Home-made jams, chutneys and pickles (relishes), honey, molasses, Barbados (raw cane) sugar, Demerara (brown) sugar, a little caster sugar for special desserts and a selection of dried fruits.

CHEESE

Cheese made with vegetarian rennet is available at most health food stores and some supermarkets.

MISCELLANEOUS

Baking powder, cream of tartar, bicarbonate of soda (baking soda), agar-agar, gelozone (vegetarian setting agent), non-fat dried milk powder and a selection of canned foods for standbys and luxuries.

Avoid buying too much of any one item unless you are really sure you will get through it quickly. There is nothing worse than looking at a mountain of beans or spaghetti and wondering if you will ever come to the end of it. These items do deteriorate over time so they are best eaten fresh.

Basic Preparation

Some of the items used in the recipes could be unfamiliar. So here is a run down on basic preparation.

PULSES

In general, dried pulses need to be soaked before cooking. This can be done overnight in cold water, or for 5 hours before they are cooked.

Whole lentils: Soak overnight. Simmer for 1 hour, then check for tenderness. Alternatively, pressure-cook for 20 minutes.

Split lentils: No soaking required. Simmer for about 30–45 minutes depending on how 'mushy' you like them. Alternatively, pressure-cook for 10 minutes.

Split peas: No soaking required. Simmer for about an hour or pressure-cook for 15 minutes.

Chick-peas and whole green peas: Soak overnight. Simmer for about $1\frac{1}{4}$ hours, then start to check the softness of the peas. Alternatively, pressure-cook for 20 minutes.

Red kidney beans, Pinto beans, Borlotti beans and Greek Foulia beans: Soak overnight. Drain thoroughly, then boil briskly in fresh water for at least 10 minutes. Simmer for a further 45 minutes and then start checking. Alternatively, pressure-cook for 15 minutes.

Haricot (navy) beans, black eye beans and butter (dried lima) beans: Soak overnight. Drain thoroughly, then boil briskly in fresh water for at least 10 minutes. Simmer for about $1\frac{1}{4}$ hours and then start checking. Alternatively, pressure-cook for 15 minutes.

Soya beans: Soak overnight in a refrigerator. Soya beans tend to start fermenting if left in a warm kitchen. Drain thoroughly, then boil briskly for at least 10 minutes. Simmer for at least 2 hours or pressure-cook for 35-40 minutes. Even when fully cooked, soya beans tend to retain a slight 'bite'.

Never add salt at the beginning of cooking as this will harden the beans; add it after cooking is completed.

Note The above instructions for soaking, draining and initial fast boiling of beans applies no matter whether the beans are cooked in a saucepan, pressure cooker, slow cooker or microwave cooker.

WHOLEMEAL (WHOLEWHEAT) FLOUR

Most of the recipes in this book have been tested with wholemeal (wholewheat) flour. I do not find that there is usually any need to change the proportions of the ingredients when substituting wholemeal (wholewheat) flour for white flour. There are, however, some recipes which may work better with 81% extraction flour. Certain cakes, choux pastry and soufflés fall into this category.

Here are one or two pointers to bear in mind when using wholemeal (wholewheat) flour:
a) Pastry made with wholemeal (wholewheat) flour tends to be extremely crumbly and can be difficult to roll out. This can be overcome by pressing the pastry into the pie or flan dish (pie pan) without rolling it out. Use your fingers to work the pastry across the base and up the sides of the dish. This method is particularly useful for sweet pastry made with wholemeal (wholewheat) flour.

Alternatively, you can add a little more water to the mixture. Provided that you leave the pastry to rest, the fibrous material in the flour will take up the moisture, leaving the pastry less sticky and easier to roll out.
b) Sauces made with wholemeal (wholewheat) flour look a little speckled. This is due to the bran in the flour and this can be sieved out if preferred.
c) Wholewheat pasta behaves in almost exactly the same way as white pasta. Ravioli dough, in particular, made with wholemeal (wholewheat) flour, rolls out extremely well.

POLENTA

Use a wire whisk when adding cornmeal to boiling water. This helps to prevent lumps forming. Alternate with a wooden spoon to get into the corners. If the mixture does go lumpy, just pass it through a sieve and continue as instructed. This note also applies to semolina and rice flour recipes.

BROWN RICE

All the recipes in the book have been tested with brown rice. This takes a little longer to cook then polished rice and has a nutty flavour. It does not usually need to be washed after cooking as the grains remain separate.

SESAME SEEDS

Unless they are being used for decoration, sesame seeds are usually ground before use. They are thought to be more digestible used in this way. To toast them, sprinkle whole sesame seeds into the base of the grill (broiler) pan, and place under the heat for 2-3 minutes until brown in colour. Do not let them burn. Grind and store in an airtight jar.

NUTS

Nuts are usually cheaper if bought whole in their brown skins, and the skins then usually removed before use. To remove skins, shake peanuts in a bag, rubbing slightly at the same time. Hazelnuts (filberts) will need 5 minutes in the oven before shaking or rubbing the skins loose. Almonds should be placed in a pan of boiling water for a minute or so, after which the skins are easily removed.

DRIED FRUITS

Raisins, currants, dates and sultanas (golden raisins) are used as they are bought. Dried bananas can be used soaked or unsoaked. Dried apricots, prunes, peaches, apples and pears usually need soaking overnight in cold water. Wash the fruit first, then use the water in which the fruit has been soaked to cook them in.

VEGETARIAN STOCK

There are a number of different types of vegetable stock which are available to the vegetarian cook, and the choice will depend upon the strength and flavour required and on how much time you have available to prepare it.

The quickest and easiest solution is to use one of the proprietary brands of vegetable or, more specifically, vegetarian stock (bouillon) cubes. Do, however, check the ingredients list before you buy, since the term 'vegetable cube' does not always mean 'vegetarian'!

Another quick method is to dissolve a little yeast (vegetable) extract in hot water. Yeast extract does, however, have a fairly distinctive flavour and this can dominate a dish. It should be used sparingly unless that is the particular flavour required.

Home-made vegetable stock takes a little longer to prepare but will be very good indeed. Keep the vegetable water from simmering or steaming vegetables, and use it as the base for a stock. Boil it up with sliced onion, carrot, celery and a few herbs. Strain and use or store in a refrigerator or freezer until required. It is quite a good idea to concentrate your vegetable stock by boiling and then freezing in ice trays. The cubes can then be stored in polythene bags and used at will.

SETTING AGENTS

Agar-agar is one vegetarian alternative to gelatine. It gives a really clear jelly but can be difficult to prepare. It is made by sprinkling into boiling water and stirring vigorously until completely dissolved. Particular care is needed to see that it does not go lumpy. If it does, it can be strained. Agar-agar starts to set very quickly after removing from the heat; so use it at once and if you need to strain it, heat the sieve first.

Gelozone is another vegetarian setting agent. It is easier

to use than agar-agar but it gives an opaque effect, and this limits its use to mousses and the like. Make into a smooth paste with cold water, then bring to the boil and simmer for 2-3 minutes before stirring into the mixture to be set.

BEAN SPROUTS

Bean sprouts are on sale in a number of shops, but it is also a very simple matter to sprout your own. Sprouting at home also means that you have a much wider choice of sprout.

The choice ranges from the mung beans of the familiar Chinese bean sprouts, chick-peas and soya beans through alfalfa seed and spicy fenugreek to special mixtures put together by the seed merchants. But do not try to sprout beans or seeds which have been sitting in your store cupboard for months–apart from chick-peas they will not sprout!

Sprouts are particularly rich in protein as well as in essential vitamins and minerals. They also contain dietary fibre and a number of enzymes which help in digestion. They are about the freshest vegetable you are ever likely to eat as they are still growing when you eat them. Even fresh garden produce loses 25% of its vitamin content within 30 minutes of being picked.

Sprouting is extremely easy. All you need to do is to soak a small amount of the seeds or beans in a large jar. Leave to stand overnight, then drain, rinse and drain again. Cover the neck of the jar with some muslin (cheesecloth) and leave on its side on the draining board. Repeat the rinsing and draining twice a day, and leave the container on its side so that the water drains away. The sprouts will be ready in 4-5 days. Do not let them grow too big as they will lose their flavour and become tough.

Sprouts are best eaten raw, but they can be lightly steamed or sautéed. Do make sure not to overcook them. Excess sprouts can be stored in a refrigerator in a closed polythene container.

DIETARY SUPPLEMENTS

Although some dietary supplements are not very palatable, they can very often be used mixed with other ingredients to mask the taste. Items to consider are:

Brewer's yeast: This is rich in vitamins of the B complex as well as having a relatively high protein content. 1 × 15ml spoon/1 tablespoon will provide 2 grams of usable protein of around 5% of your total daily requirements. The amino acid pattern also makes it a good complementary mix for nuts and cereals.

Wheatgerm: This has a similar protein content to brewer's yeast and is rich in Vitamin E, though the general level of vitamins and minerals is nothing like as good.

Wheat bran: This can be added to soups and cereals to improve the fibre content of the diet.

Freezing Vegetarian Food

The freezer is just as useful to the vegetarian cook as it is to the general cook. The way you use it will, of course, depend on your life-style and on the kind of food that you and your family prefer. However, there are some things that it is extremely convenient to have readily available in the freezer. These include cooked rice, cooked beans of various kinds, grated cheese, prepared breadcrumbs, pastry, fruit purées, batter and pancake mixes, bread and rolls, basic sauces, herbs, grated orange and lemon rind and stock.

Starting Off

Shropska

Metric/imperial		American
	4 large tomatoes, coarsely chopped	
	1 small onion, coarsely chopped	
	$\frac{1}{2}$ green pepper, de-seeded and coarsely chopped	
	10cm/4 inch length cucumber, coarsely chopped	
	3 sticks celery, coarsely chopped	
	salt, freshly ground pepper	
100g/4 oz	hard cheese, grated	1 cup
	juice of 1 lemon	

Layer the vegetables in four individual bowls, then top with salt and pepper, the grated cheese and lemon juice. Chill for 30–45 minutes before serving.

Melon and Cucumber Salad

Metric/imperial		American
	$\frac{1}{2}$ honeydew melon, diced	
	7.5cm/3 inch length cucumber, diced	
	3 sprigs mint, finely chopped	
1 × 15ml spoon/ 1 tablespoon	yoghurt	1 tablespoon
1 × 15ml spoon/ 1 tablespoon	mayonnaise	1 tablespoon
	salt, freshly ground pepper	
	GARNISH sprigs mint	

Mix together the melon and cucumber with the mint, yoghurt, mayonnaise and seasoning. Put into individual bowls, and garnish with sprigs of mint.

Shropska

EGG AND TARRAGON MOUSSE

Metric/imperial		American
150ml/¼ pint	double (heavy) cream	⅔ cup
	4 hard-boiled (hard-cooked) eggs	
2 × 5ml spoons/ 2 teaspoons	gelozone (vegetarian setting agent)	2 teaspoons
4 × 15ml spoons/ 4 tablespoons	water	5 tablespoons
3 × 15ml spoons/ 3 tablespoons	yoghurt	4 tablespoons
2 × 5ml spoons/ 2 teaspoons	dried tarragon	2 teaspoons
	a few drops Tabasco (hot pepper) sauce	
	salt, freshly ground pepper	

Whip the cream until fairly stiff. Sieve the eggs, reserving four slices for the garnish. Mix together the eggs and cream. Blend the gelozone (setting agent) and water to form a paste, then heat to boiling point and simmer for 2–3 minutes. Add to the egg and cream mixture, then add the yoghurt, 1 × 5ml spoon/1 teaspoon tarragon, the Tabasco (hot pepper) sauce and seasoning; mix well together.

Pour the mixture into individual ramekin dishes, and garnish with a slice of the reserved sliced egg. Chill for at least 2 hours before serving. Garnish with the remaining tarragon.

Serve with hot toast.

ARTICHOKES WITH RENAISSANCE SAUCE

Metric/imperial		American
	4 globe artichokes	
	lemon juice	
	SAUCE salt, freshly ground pepper	
300ml/½ pint	yoghurt	1¼ cups
1 × 15ml spoon/ 1 tablespoon	concentrated tomato purée (paste)	1 tablespoon
	1 small onion, chopped	
1 × 5ml spoon/ 1 teaspoon	dill seed	1 teaspoon
	GARNISH paprika	

Cook the artichokes in boiling salted water with a little lemon juice for about 45 minutes until the leaves come away easily. Remove the centre leaves and the choke, drain, then leave to cool.

To make the sauce, stir together the seasoning, yoghurt, tomato purée (paste), chopped onion and the dill seed. Spoon into the centre of each artichoke, and sprinkle with paprika just before serving.

PEANUT AND GARLIC PÂTÉ

Metric/imperial		American
3 × 15ml spoons/ 3 tablespoons	peanut butter	4 tablespoons
100g/4 oz	quark (low-fat soft cheese)	$\frac{1}{2}$ cup
	2 cloves garlic, finely chopped	
2 × 15ml spoons/ 2 tablespoons	Tabasco (hot pepper) sauce	3 tablespoons
	salt, freshly ground pepper	

Mix together the peanut butter, cheese, garlic and Tabasco (hot pepper) sauce until smooth, then season to taste. Put into four individual dishes, and chill for 1 hour.

Serve with crusty French bread.

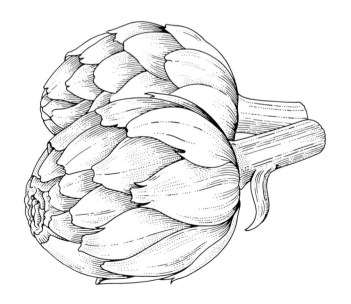

GREEN PEA SOUFFLÉ

Metric/imperial		American
1 × 5ml spoon/ 1 teaspoon	gelozone (vegetarian setting agent)	1 teaspoon
300ml/$\frac{1}{2}$ pint	water	1$\frac{1}{4}$ cups
1 × 2.5ml spoon/ $\frac{1}{4}$ teaspoon	yeast (vegetable) extract	$\frac{1}{4}$ teaspoon
225g/8 oz	fresh peas	1$\frac{1}{2}$ cups
4 × 15ml spoons/ 4 tablespoons	double (heavy) cream	5 tablespoons
	1 egg white	

Blend the gelozone (setting agent) and a little water to form a paste, then heat to boiling point, and simmer for 2–3 minutes.

Dissolve the yeast (vegetable) extract in the remaining water, and heat to boiling point. Add the peas, then cook for 8–10 minutes until tender. Leave to cool.

Pass the peas through a sieve, or process in a blender or food processor. Whip the cream until stiff, then whisk the egg white separately until stiff. Add the cream to the puréed peas, then stir in the dissolved gelozone (setting agent). Mix well, then fold in the egg white. Pour into individual ramekin dishes, and chill for 3–4 hours.

Serve with brown bread and butter.

SAVOURY STUFFED APPLES

Metric/imperial		American
	2 large cooking apples, halved and cored	
50g/2 oz	wholemeal (wholewheat) breadcrumbs	1 cup
25g/1 oz	ground peanuts	$\frac{1}{4}$ cup
	1 small onion, finely chopped	
2 × 5ml spoons/ 2 teaspoons	toasted ground sesame seeds	2 teaspoons
2 × 5ml spoons/ 2 teaspoons	concentrated tomato purée (paste)	2 teaspoons
1 × 2.5ml spoon/ $\frac{1}{2}$ teaspoon	dried oregano	$\frac{1}{2}$ teaspoon
150ml/$\frac{1}{4}$ pint	tomato juice	$\frac{2}{3}$ cup
	salt, freshly ground pepper	

Slice each apple half into two layers, and place four slices in an ovenproof dish. Mix together the breadcrumbs and other ingredients, and use half to cover the apple slices. Place another layer of apple on top and finish off with the remaining stuffing. Cook in a fairly hot oven, 200°C/400°F/Gas 6, for 1 hour until the apples are tender.

CHICK-PEAS À LA GRECQUE

Metric/imperial		American
100g/4 oz	chick-peas	generous $\frac{1}{2}$ cup
1 × 15ml spoon/ 1 tablespoon	cooking oil	1 tablespoon
	2 small onions, thinly sliced	
100g/4 oz	button mushrooms	1 cup
600ml/1 pint	white wine	2$\frac{1}{2}$ cups
2 × 5ml spoons/ 2 teaspoons	concentrated tomato pureé (paste)	2 teaspoons
1 × 2.5ml spoon/ $\frac{1}{2}$ teaspoon	dried oregano	$\frac{1}{2}$ teaspoon
	1 bay leaf	
	salt, freshly ground pepper	

Soak the chick-peas overnight in cold water, then cook for about 1$\frac{1}{4}$ hours until almost cooked; drain well.

Heat the oil in a pan, and cook the onions until transparent. Add the mushrooms and chick-peas, then pour over the wine, and add the tomato pureé (paste), herbs and seasoning. Heat to boiling point, then simmer for 30 minutes. Serve chilled.

Potato and Mushroom Celeste (page 39) **and** *Chick-peas à la Grecque*

PIQUANT ONIONS

Metric/imperial		American
25g/1 oz	butter **or** margarine	2 tablespoons
450g/1 lb	onions, sliced	1 lb
1 × 5ml spoon/ 1 teaspoon	concentrated tomato purée (paste)	1 teaspoon
½ × 2.5ml spoon/ ¼ teaspoon	chilli powder	¼ teaspoon
	a few drops Tabasco (hot pepper) sauce	
2 × 5ml spoons/ 2 teaspoons	vinegar	2 teaspoons
1 × 5ml spoon/ 1 teaspoon	soy sauce	1 teaspoon
	salt, freshly ground pepper	
	GARNISH chopped parsley	

Melt the butter in a pan, and cook the onions until transparent. Add the other ingredients, and cook for a further 15 minutes or until the onions are soft. Serve in individual ramekin dishes, and sprinkle with chopped parsley.

STUFFED ONIONS WITH SOYA AND ROSEMARY

Metric/imperial		American
	4 large onions	
100g/4 oz	ground cooked soya beans	½ cup
1 × 5ml spoon/ 1 teaspoon	dried rosemary	1 teaspoon
	salt, freshly ground pepper	
	butter **or** margarine	

Steam the onions for 5–8 minutes to soften them, then drain and remove the centres; chop them finely. Mix with the soya beans, rosemary and the seasoning. Spoon the mixture back into the centres of the onions, then put the onions on a heatproof plate, and dot with flakes of butter. Brown under a hot grill (broiler) for 5–8 minutes.

SPINACH GNOCCHI

Metric/imperial		American
675g/1½ lb	fresh leaf spinach	1½ lb
25g/1 oz	butter **or** margarine	2 tablespoons
	milk	
40g/1½ oz	semolina	¼ cup
	salt, freshly ground pepper	
2 × 15ml spoons/ 2 tablespoons	Parmesan cheese, grated	3 tablespoons
	SAUCE	
25g/1 oz	butter **or** margarine	2 tablespoons
25g/1 oz	wholemeal (wholewheat) flour, sifted	¼ cup
450ml/¾ pint	milk	2 cups
100g/4 oz	quark (low-fat soft cheese)	½ cup
½ × 2.5ml spoon/ ¼ teaspoon	celery seed **or** celery salt	¼ teaspoon

Cook the spinach with a little butter until soft. Drain, retaining the liquid and make this up to 450ml/¾ pint/ 2 US cups with milk. Put into a pan with the remaining butter and the semolina, and heat to boiling point, stirring all the time. Add the spinach and salt, and cook for a further 10–15 minutes, stirring occasionally. Transfer to a bowl and leave to cool.

Meanwhile, prepare the sauce. Melt the butter in a pan, stir in the flour over low heat, then add the milk, and cook until the sauce thickens, stirring all the time. Stir in the quark, and season to taste with salt, pepper and celery seed or salt.

Place rounded spoonfuls of the cooled gnocchi mixture in individual ovenproof dishes, and cover with the sauce. Sprinkle with Parmesan cheese, and cook in a fairly hot oven, 200°C/400°F/Gas 6, for 15–20 minutes until browned.

LOVE APPLES

Metric/imperial		American
	4 good-sized tomatoes, skinned and sliced	
	sherry	
	salt, freshly ground pepper	
1 × 15ml spoon/ 1 tablespoon	hard cheese, grated	1 tablespoon
4 × 15ml spoons/ 4 tablespoons	double (heavy) cream	5 tablespoons

Place the tomato slices in individual ramekin dishes, cover with sherry, then season to taste. Cook in a fairly hot oven, 190°C/375°F/Gas 5, for 20 minutes, then sprinkle with the grated cheese and cream, and cook for a further 2–3 minutes just until the cream and cheese have melted. Serve at once.

SOUPED UP

BARLEY BROTH

Metric/imperial		American
50g/2 oz	dried haricot (navy) beans	scant $\frac{1}{4}$ cup
1 × 15ml spoon/ 1 tablespoon	cooking oil	1 tablespoon
	1 large onion, finely chopped	
25g/1 oz	pearl barley	2 tablespoons
50g/2 oz	lentils	$\frac{1}{4}$ cup
1.2 litres/ 2 pints	vegetable stock	5 cups
	dried thyme	
	bay leaf	
	salt, freshly ground pepper	
1 × 15ml spoon/ 1 tablespoon	concentrated tomato purée (paste)	1 tablespoon

GARNISH
chopped parsley

Soak the beans overnight in cold water, then drain, discarding the water. Boil briskly in fresh water for at least 10 minutes, then drain.

Meanwhile, heat the oil in a pan, and cook the onion until soft. Add the barley and lentils, then pour on the stock. Sprinkle with the herbs and seasoning, then add the beans and tomato purée (paste). Heat to boiling point, then simmer for $1\frac{1}{2}$–2 hours. Garnish with chopped parsley.

CREAM OF CHICK-PEA SOUP

Metric/imperial		American
175g/6 oz	chick-peas	scant 1 cup
750ml/1$\frac{1}{4}$ pints	vegetable stock	3 cups
	black pepper	
2 × 15ml spoons/ 2 tablespoons	double (heavy) cream	3 tablespoons

Soak the chick-peas overnight in cold water. Drain, then put into a pan with the stock, and simmer for $1\frac{1}{4}$ hours until cooked. Pass through a sieve or process in a blender or food processor. Add the black pepper and then the cream. Re-heat without boiling.

Serve with fried wholemeal (wholewheat) bread croûtons.

Barley Broth

MIXED PULSE SOUP

Metric/imperial		American
50g/2 oz	red kidney beans	scant $\frac{1}{4}$ cup
25g/1 oz	chick-peas	1 tablespoon
25g/1 oz	lentils	$1\frac{1}{2}$ tablespoons
	1 onion	
900ml/1½ pints	water	$3\frac{3}{4}$ cups
1 × 5ml spoon/ 1 teaspoon	fresh mint, chopped	1 teaspoon
$\frac{1}{2}$ × 2.5ml spoon/ $\frac{1}{4}$ teaspoon	ground cumin	$\frac{1}{4}$ teaspoon
	a pinch of turmeric	
	salt, freshly ground pepper	
50g/2 oz	green vegetables (spinach, cabbage or lettuce) chopped	$\frac{2}{3}$ cup
	GARNISH chopped parsley	

Soak the beans, chick-peas and lentils separately overnight in cold water. Drain, discarding the water, then boil the beans briskly in fresh water for at least 10 minutes; drain well.

Place the beans, chick-peas and lentils in a pan with the onion, water, mint, cumin, turmeric and seasoning. Heat to boiling point, then simmer for 1–2 hours until all the vegetables are soft. Add the green vegetables 15 minutes before serving, then pass through a sieve or process in a blender or food processor. Re-heat until hot. Garnish with chopped parsley.

DUTCH PEA SOUP

Metric/imperial		American
1 × 15ml spoon/ 1 tablespoon	cooking oil	1 tablespoon
	2 large onions, sliced	
225g/8 oz	split peas	1 cup
1.2 litres/ 2 pints	water	5 cups
1 × 5ml spoon/ 1 teaspoon	yeast (vegetable) extract	1 teaspoon
	a sprinkling of ground nutmeg	
	salt, freshly ground pepper	
	GARNISH chopped parsley	

Heat the oil in a pan, and cook the onions until browned. Add the peas, water, yeast (vegetable) extract and a sprinkling of nutmeg. Season to taste, then heat to boiling point. Simmer for about 1½ hours until cooked. Pass through a sieve or process in a blender or food processor, then re-heat until hot. Garnish with chopped parsley.

Serve with Nut Dumplings (page 57).

TOMATO, CAULIFLOWER AND TARRAGON SOUP

Metric/imperial		American
25g/1 oz	butter **or** margarine	2 tablespoons
	1 medium onion, chopped	
5 × 15ml spoons/ 5 tablespoons	sherry	6 tablespoons
225g/8 oz	cauliflower florets	$1\frac{1}{3}$ cups
225g/8 oz	tomatoes, chopped	1 cup
750ml/$1\frac{1}{4}$ pints	vegetable stock	3 cups
1 × 2.5ml spoon/ $\frac{1}{2}$ teaspoon	sugar	$\frac{1}{2}$ teaspoon
1–2 × 5ml spoons/ 1–2 teaspoons	dried tarragon	1–2 teaspoons
	salt, freshly ground pepper	

Melt the butter in a pan, and cook the onion until golden. Add the sherry, then heat to boiling point. Add the cauliflower, tomatoes, vegetable stock, sugar and half the tarragon, and season to taste. Bring to the boil, then simmer for 45 minutes. Pass through a sieve or process in a blender or food processor. Season to taste, then re-heat until hot. Sprinkle with the remaining tarragon before serving.

COUNTRY VEGETABLE SOUP

Metric/imperial		American
25g/1 oz	butter **or** margarine	2 tablespoons
	2 onions, chopped	
450g/1 lb	mixed vegetables, coarsely chopped (see **Note**)	1 lb
900ml/$1\frac{1}{2}$ pints	vegetable stock	$3\frac{3}{4}$ cups
1 × 5ml spoon/ 1 teaspoon	yeast (vegetable) extract	1 teaspoon
	1 bay leaf	
1 × 2.5ml spoon/ $\frac{1}{2}$ teaspoon	dried marjoram	$\frac{1}{2}$ teaspoon
$\frac{1}{2}$ × 2.5 ml spoon/ $\frac{1}{4}$ teaspoon	dried thyme	$\frac{1}{4}$ teaspoon
	salt, freshly ground pepper	

Melt the butter in a pan, and cook the onions until soft. Add the mixed vegetables, then cook for a further 5 minutes. Add the stock, yeast (vegetable) extract, herbs and seasoning, then heat to boiling point and simmer for 1 hour. Pass through a sieve or process in a blender or food processor. Season to taste, then re-heat until boiling.

Note Use carrots, leeks, potatoes, celery and turnip.

COURGETTE AND DILL SOUP

Metric/imperial		American
25g/1 oz	butter **or** margarine	2 tablespoons
	1 onion, chopped	
5 × 15ml spoons/ 5 tablespoons	sherry	6 tablespoons
450g/1 lb	courgettes (zucchini), coarsely chopped	1 lb
1 × 5ml spoon/ 1 teaspoon	dill seed	1 teaspoon
750ml/1¼ pints	vegetable stock	3 cups
	salt, freshly ground pepper	
4 × 15ml spoons/ 4 tablespoons	double (heavy) cream	5 tablespoons

Melt the butter in a pan, and cook the onion until transparent. Add the sherry, then heat to boiling point. Add the courgettes (zucchini), dill seed, stock and seasoning, then bring back to the boil and simmer for 45 minutes. Pass through a sieve or process in a blender or food processor. Season to taste, then re-heat until boiling. Serve with a spoon of cream in each bowl.

ICED CUCUMBER SOUP

Metric/imperial		American
50g/2 oz	butter **or** margarine	¼ cup
	1 onion, chopped	
150ml/¼ pint	white wine	⅔ cup
225g/8 oz	potatoes, peeled and sliced	1⅓ cups
	5cm/2 inch length cucumber, diced	
600ml/1 pint	vegetable stock	2½ cups
	salt, freshly ground pepper	
4 × 15ml spoons/ 4 tablespoons	GARNISH single (light) cream	5 tablespoons
	chopped parsley	
	2.5cm/1 inch length cucumber, diced	

Melt the butter in a pan, and cook the onion until golden. Add the wine, then heat to boiling point. Add the potatoes, half the cucumber, the stock and seasoning, then simmer for 30 minutes. Leave to cool.

Pass the soup through a sieve or process in a blender or food processor, then season to taste. Serve chilled, garnished with the cream, chopped parsley and the remaining cucumber.

Iced Cucumber Soup

JERUSALEM ARTICHOKE SOUP

Metric/imperial		American
1 × 15ml spoon/ 1 tablespoon	cooking oil	1 tablespoon
	2 leeks, sliced	
450g/1 lb	Jerusalem artichokes, peeled and sliced	1 lb
	1 large potato, peeled and sliced	
300ml/½ pint	milk	1¼ cups
300ml/½ pint	vegetable stock	1¼ cups
	1 bay leaf	
½ × 2.5ml spoon/ ¼ teaspoon	dried marjoram	¼ teaspoon

GARNISH
chopped parsley

Heat the oil in a pan, and cook the leeks for 2–3 minutes to release their flavour. Add the artichokes and sliced potato, then cover with the milk, stock and herbs, and simmer for 20 minutes. Serve the soup as it is; alternatively, pass through a sieve or process in a blender or food processor, then re-heat until hot. Sprinkle with chopped parsley before serving.

CREOLE NUT SOUP

Metric/imperial		American
25g/1 oz	butter **or** margarine	2 tablespoons
	2 medium onions, finely chopped	
	4 sticks celery, finely chopped	
2 × 5ml spoons/ 2 teaspoons	concentrated tomato purée (paste)	2 teaspoons
2 × 15ml spoons/ 2 tablespoons	wholemeal (wholewheat) flour	3 tablespoons
	salt, freshly ground pepper	
3 × 15ml spoons/ 3 tablespoons	peanut butter	4 tablespoons
300ml/½ pint	milk	1¼ cups
600ml/1 pint	tomato juice	2½ cups

GARNISH
sprigs watercress

Melt the butter in a pan, and cook the onions and celery until soft. Add the tomato purée (paste) and flour, then season to taste. Blend in the peanut butter, then add the milk gradually, stirring all the time. Heat to boiling point, then add the tomato juice. Re-heat until boiling, and serve at once, garnished with sprigs of watercress.

Hungarian Apple Soup

Metric/imperial		American
1 × 15ml spoon/ 1 tablespoon	cooking oil	1 tablespoon
	2 onions, chopped	
	1 clove of garlic, crushed	
	4 eating apples, chopped	
	1 red pepper, de-seeded and chopped	
	2 large gherkins **or** 1 pickled cucumber (dill pickle), chopped	
600ml/1 pint	vegetable stock	2½ cups
1 × 2.5ml spoon/ ½ teaspoon	paprika	½ teaspoon
1 × 2.5ml spoon/ ½ teaspoon	Muscovado (raw cane) sugar	½ teaspoon
1–2 × 15ml spoons/ 1–2 tablespoons	fresh chives, chopped	1–3 tablespoons
100ml/4 fl oz	soured cream	½ cup

Heat the oil in a pan, and cook the onions, garlic, apples, pepper and gherkins for 3–4 minutes. Add the stock, paprika, sugar and half the chives, then heat to boiling point and simmer for 20 minutes. Stir in the soured cream, and serve sprinkled with more chives.

Apple and Celery Soup

Metric/imperial		American
1 × 15ml spoon/ 1 tablepoon	cooking oil	1 tablespoon
	1 onion, chopped	
3 × 15ml spoons/ 3 tablespoons	sherry	4 tablespoons
225g/8 oz	cooking apples, peeled and chopped	2 cups
225g/8 oz	celery, chopped	2 cups
750ml/1¼ pints	water	3 cups
1 × 2.5ml spoon/ ½ teaspoon	ground cumin	½ teaspoon
	salt, freshly ground pepper	
3 × 15ml spoons/ 3 tablespoons	soured cream	4 tablespoons

GARNISH
ratafias

Heat the oil in a pan, and cook the onion until soft. Add the sherry, then heat to boiling point. Add the apples, celery and water, then sprinkle with the cumin, and season to taste. Bring to the boil, then simmer for 45 minutes. Pass through a sieve or process in a blender or food processor. Mix in the soured cream, then re-heat before serving. Do not boil. Garnish with ratafias just before serving.

THE CENTRE PIECE

SWEETCORN EGG NESTS

Metric/imperial		American
450g/1 lb	potatoes (see **Note**)	1 lb
225g/8 oz	sweetcorn kernels	1½ cups
	4 eggs	
1 × 5ml spoon/ 1 teaspoon	dried tarragon	1 teaspoon
	salt, freshly ground pepper	
15g/½ oz	butter **or** margarine	1 tablespoon

Parboil the potatoes for 15 minutes, then peel and slice, and lay in four buttered individual ovenproof dishes. Sprinkle the sweetcorn round the edges to form a nest. Crack one egg into the centre of each nest, and sprinkle with tarragon and salt and pepper. Dot with flakes of butter. Bake in a hot oven, 220°C/425°F/Gas 7, for 15 minutes until browned.

Note Leftover potatoes can be used.

JERUSALEM EGGS

Metric/imperial		American
450g/1 lb	Jerusalem artichokes, peeled	1 lb
450g/1 lb	potatoes	1 lb
75g/3 oz	butter **or** margarine	6 tablespoons
	salt, freshly ground pepper	
	8 hard-boiled (hard-cooked) eggs, halved	
50g/2 oz	wholemeal (wholewheat) flour, sifted	½ cup
300ml/½ pint	milk	1¼ cups

Steam the artichokes for about 10 minutes until cooked through. Boil the potatoes, then mash with 25g/1 oz/2 US tablespoons butter, three-quarters of the artichokes, and the salt and pepper. Put to one side.

Remove the yolks, and mash them with the remaining artichokes. Season to taste, then pile the mixture back into the egg whites. Place in a casserole.

Melt the remaining butter in a pan, stir in the flour over low heat, then add the milk, and cook until the sauce thickens, stirring all the time. Season to taste.

Pour the sauce over the eggs, then spoon the reserved potato and artichoke mixture round the edge of the dish, and bake in a hot oven, 220°C/425°F/Gas 7, for 20 minutes until cooked.

South American Baked Eggs

Metric/imperial		American
1 × 15ml spoon/ 1 tablespoon	cooking oil	1 tablespoon
	4 onions, finely chopped	
	1 green pepper, de-seeded and finely chopped	
350g/12 oz	cooked red beans, mashed	$\frac{3}{4}$ lb
1 × 15ml spoon/ 1 tablespoon	dried thyme	1 tablespoon
	salt, freshly ground pepper	
	4 eggs	
4 × 15ml spoons/ 4 tablespoons	red wine	5 tablespoons

Heat the oil in a pan, and cook the onions and pepper until the onions are transparent. Mix in the beans, then add the thyme and seasoning, and spoon into an ovenproof dish. Make four wells, and break an egg into each one. Pour over the wine, then cook in a hot oven, 220°C/425°F/Gas 7, for about 15–20 minutes or until the eggs are set.

Hot Cauliflower Mousse

Metric/imperial		American
	1 large cauliflower, broken into florets	
25g/1 oz	butter **or** margarine	2 tablespoons
25g/1 oz	wholemeal (wholewheat) flour	$\frac{1}{4}$ cup
10 × 5ml spoons/ 10 teaspoons	white wine **or** dry sherry	10 teaspoons
175ml/6 fl oz	vegetable stock (see **Note**)	$\frac{3}{4}$ cup
175ml/6 fl oz	milk	$\frac{3}{4}$ cup
	ground cinnamon	
	salt, freshly ground pepper	
	2 eggs, beaten	

Steam the cauliflower for 15 minutes, then drain, retaining the liquid to include in vegetable stock. Rub the cauliflower through a sieve or process in a blender or food processor.

Melt the butter in a pan, stir in the flour over low heat, then add the wine or sherry and the stock and milk. Cook gently, stirring all the time until thickened, then add the cinnamon, and season to taste. Remove from the heat, add the eggs and the puréed cauliflower, and pour into a 600ml/1 pint/2$\frac{1}{2}$ US cup greased soufflé dish. Cook in a hot oven, 200°C/400°F/Gas 6, in a baking tin (pan) filled with 5cm/2 inches water for 1 hour until the mousse is set.

Note The vegetable stock can be made with the water used to steam the cauliflower.

CARDAMOM CHEESE PIE

Metric/imperial		American
50g/2 oz	butter **or** margarine	4 tablespoons
125g/5 oz	wholemeal (wholewheat) flour, sifted	1¼ cups
	salt	
100g/4 oz	hard cheese, grated	1 cup
100g/4 oz	raisins	⅔ cup
	4 hard-boiled (hard-cooked) eggs, chopped	
1 × 15ml spoon/ 1 tablespoon	sugar	1 tablespoon
	1 cardamom seed, crushed	

Rub (cut in) the fat into the flour and salt, and bind with water. Roll out on a lightly floured surface and use three-quarters to line one 20cm/8 inch pie dish. Use the remaining pastry to form a pastry lid.

Mix together the cheese, raisins, eggs, sugar and cardamom seed, and spoon into the pastry case (pie shell). Cover with the pastry lid, then crimp the edges and prick the centre. Bake in a fairly hot oven, 200°C/400°F/Gas 6, for 45 minutes or until the pastry is cooked.

MALI PIE

Metric/imperial		American
1 × 15ml spoon/ 1 tablespoon	cooking oil	1 tablespoon
175g/6 oz	onions, sliced	1½ cups
175g/6 oz	ground roasted peanuts	1½ cups
	6 fresh tomatoes, skinned and chopped	
	a few drops Tabasco (hot pepper) sauce	
1 × 15ml spoon/ 1 tablespoon	dried marjoram	1 tablespoon
	salt	
50g/2 oz	butter **or** margarine	¼ cup
125g/5 oz	wholemeal (wholewheat) flour, sifted	1¼ cups

Heat the oil in a pan, and cook the onions until soft and brown. Stir in the peanuts, tomatoes, a few drops of Tabasco (hot pepper) sauce, the marjoram and salt to taste. Boil for 2–3 minutes to reduce the liquid, then leave to cool.

Meanwhile, rub (cut in) the fat into the flour and salt, and bind with water. Roll out on a lightly floured surface and use three-quarters to line one 20cm/8 inch pie dish. Use the remaining pastry to form a pastry lid.

Place the peanut mixture in the pastry case (pie shell), then cover with the pastry lid. Crimp the edges and prick the centre. Bake in a fairly hot oven, 200°C/400°F/Gas 6, for about 45 minutes or until the pastry is cooked.

COURGETTE AND OATMEAL SAVOURY

Metric/imperial		American
2 × 15ml spoons/ 2 tablespoons	cooking oil	3 tablespoons
	2 large onions, finely chopped	
4 × 15ml spoons/ 4 tablespoons	medium oatmeal	5 tablespoons
	salt, freshly ground pepper	
150ml/$\frac{1}{4}$ pint	vegetable stock	$\frac{2}{3}$ cup
450g/1 lb	courgettes (zucchini), sliced	1 lb
	4 tomatoes, skinned and sliced	
	4 eggs, beaten	
75g/3 oz	hard cheese, grated	$\frac{3}{4}$ cup

Heat 1 × 15ml spoon/1 tablespoon oil in a pan, and cook the onions until golden. Add the oatmeal, then cook for a further 2–3 minutes. Add the seasoning and the stock, stirring all the time, and cook for a further 10 minutes until the mixture thickens.

Heat the remaining oil in a second pan, and cook the courgettes (zucchini) until half cooked, then transfer them to an ovenproof dish and add the tomatoes.

Mix the eggs with the oatmeal mixture, then stir in most of the cheese, and pour this over the vegetables. Top with the remaining cheese, then cook in a fairly hot oven, 190°C/375°F/Gas 5, for about 45 minutes. Check the centre is cooked through before serving.

BEAN AND POTATO LYONNAISE

Metric/imperial		American
1 × 15ml spoon/ 1 tablespoon	cooking oil	1 tablespoon
	1 large onion, sliced	
350g/12 oz	cooked potatoes, sliced	$\frac{3}{4}$ lb
175g/6 oz	cooked dried beans	1 cup
1 × 5ml spoon/ 1 teaspoon	dried marjoram	1 teaspoon
	salt, freshly ground pepper	
1 × 15ml spoon/ 1 tablespoon	concentrated tomato purée (paste)	1 tablespoon

Heat the oil in a pan, and cook the onion until transparent. Add the sliced potatoes, then cook for 5 minutes. Add the beans, and continue cooking gently until all the ingredients are heated through. Sprinkle with the marjoram and salt and pepper to taste, then add the tomato purée (paste) mixed with a little water to give a creamy consistency. Toss the vegetables over heat in the tomato mixture until very hot. Serve at once.

FENNEL BEAN POT

Metric/imperial		American
50g/2 oz	haricot (navy) beans	$\frac{1}{4}$ cup
50g/2 oz	black eye beans	$\frac{1}{4}$ cup
50g/2 oz	butter (dried lima) beans	$\frac{1}{3}$ cup
50g/2 oz	Borlotti beans	$\frac{1}{4}$ cup
1 × 15ml spoon/ 1 tablespoon	cooking oil	1 tablespoon
	2 onions, thinly sliced	
	2 cloves garlic, crushed	
1 × 2.5ml spoon/ $\frac{1}{2}$ teaspoon	fennel seed	$\frac{1}{2}$ teaspoon
1 × 5ml spoon/ 1 teaspoon	fresh chervil **or** parsley, chopped	1 teaspoon
	salt, freshly ground pepper	
300ml/$\frac{1}{2}$ pint	red wine	$1\frac{1}{4}$ cups
	chopped parsley	

Soak the beans overnight in cold water, then drain, discarding the water. Boil the beans briskly in fresh water for at least 10 minutes, then drain well.

Heat the oil in a pan, and cook the onions and garlic until golden. Add the beans, and mix with the herbs and seasoning. Transfer to an earthenware casserole, and pour in the wine. Cover, and cook in a fairly hot oven, 190°C/375°F/Gas 5, for $1\frac{1}{4}$ hours. Increase the heat to 200°C/400°F/Gas 6, and cook for a further 40–45 minutes, stirring from time to time. Garnish with chopped parsley.

BUTTER BEAN COUNTRY CASSEROLE

Metric/imperial		American
175g/6 oz	butter (dried lima) beans	1 cup
1 × 15ml spoon/ 1 tablespoon	cooking oil	1 tablespoon
	4 small onions, thinly sliced	
350g/12 oz	mushrooms, sliced	$\frac{3}{4}$ lb
	6–8 tomatoes, chopped	
	salt, freshly ground pepper	
100g/4 oz	hard cheese, grated	1 cup
100g/4 oz	wholemeal (wholewheat) breadcrumbs	2 cups

Soak the beans overnight in cold water, then drain, discarding the water. Boil briskly in fresh water for at least 10 minutes, then cook for about $1\frac{1}{4}$ hours until almost tender; drain well.

Heat the oil in a pan, and cook the onions until transparent. Add the mushrooms, and cook for a further 5–6 minutes. Add the beans and tomatoes, then season to taste and heat through. Put into an ovenproof dish, and sprinkle with the cheese and breadcrumbs. Brown under a hot grill (broiler), and serve at once.

Butter Bean County Casserole **and** *Dutch Pea Soup (page 26) with Nut Dumplings (page 57)*

LENTIL RISOTTO WITH CHEESY TOMATOES

Metric/imperial		American
1 × 15ml spoon/ 1 tablespoon	cooking oil	1 tablespoon
	2 onions, thinly sliced	
1 × 5ml spoon/ 1 teaspoon	ground cumin seed	1 teaspoon
175g/6 oz	brown rice	scant 1 cup
100g/4 oz	lentils	$\frac{1}{2}$ cup
750ml/1$\frac{1}{4}$ pints	vegetable stock	3 cups
	salt, freshly ground pepper	
50g/2 oz	hard cheese, grated	$\frac{1}{2}$ cup
	4 tomatoes, halved	

Heat the oil in a pan, and cook the onions for 5 minutes with the cumin seed. Add the rice and lentils, and cook for a further 2–3 minutes. Add the stock and seasoning, and heat to boiling point, then simmer for about 1 hour until all the liquid is absorbed.

Meanwhile, pile the cheese on to the halved tomatoes, and place under a hot grill (broiler) until the cheese begins to brown.

Serve the risotto with the cheesy tomatoes.

AVOCADO RISOTTO

Metric/imperial		American
50g/2 oz	butter **or** margarine	$\frac{1}{4}$ cup
	1 large onion, finely chopped	
350g/12 oz	long-grain brown rice	1$\frac{2}{3}$ cups
300ml/$\frac{1}{2}$ pint	white wine	1$\frac{1}{4}$ cups
50g/2 oz	raisins	$\frac{1}{3}$ cup
1 × 2.5ml spoon/ $\frac{1}{2}$ teaspoon	fresh herbs, chopped	$\frac{1}{2}$ teaspoon
	salt, freshly ground pepper	
	2 avocado pears, peeled and chopped	
600ml/1 pint	vegetable stock	2$\frac{1}{2}$ cups

Melt the butter in a pan, and cook the onion until transparent. Add the rice, and cook gently for 3–4 minutes. Add the wine and raisins, heat to boiling point, then simmer for about 15 minutes until all the wine is absorbed, stirring occasionally. Add the herbs, seasoning, chopped avocado and the stock, then cook for about 20–30 minutes until the rice has absorbed all the stock. Add more stock if the rice shows signs of drying out too much.

Serve with Mexican Sauce (page 67).

STUFFED AVOCADO PEARS IN TOMATO SAUCE

Metric/imperial		American
450g/1 lb	tomatoes, chopped	1 lb
350ml/12 fl oz	water	1½ cups
2 × 15ml spoons/ 2 tablespoons	concentrated tomato purée (paste)	3 tablespoons
	salt, freshly ground pepper	
100g/4 oz	cream cheese	½ cup
1 × 5ml spoon/ 1 teaspoon	basil	1 teaspoon
	4 avocado pears, peeled, halved and stoned (pitted)	

Put the tomatoes into a pan with the water, tomato purée (paste) and the seasoning. Heat to boiling point, then simmer for 15–20 minutes. Pass through a sieve or process in a blender or food processor. Put to one side.

Mix together the cheese, basil and plenty of salt and pepper. Stuff the centre of each avocado pear half with the cheese mixture, then put the halves together again, and fix with a cocktail stick (tooth pick).

Put the avocado pears into a casserole, and pour over the sauce. Cover, and cook in a fairly hot oven, 200°C/400°F/Gas 6, for 20–30 minutes until the avocado pears and sauce are heated through.

POTATO AND MUSHROOM CELESTE

Metric/imperial		American
675g/1½ lb	potatoes, peeled and sliced	1½ lb
	3 onions, sliced	
	4 tomatoes, skinned and sliced	
225g/8 oz	cup mushrooms, sliced	2 cups
225g/8 oz	Brie	½ lb
1 × 5ml spoon/ 1 teaspoon	summer savory	1 teaspoon
1 × 2.5ml spoons/ ½ teaspoon	garlic salt	½ teaspoon
	salt, freshly ground pepper	
150ml/¼ pint	double (heavy) cream	⅔ cup

Layer the vegetables and cheese in a casserole, then sprinkle the layers with herbs and seasoning. Finish off with a layer of potatoes, then pour the cream over the top. Cover, and cook in a fairly hot oven, 200°C/400°F/Gas 6, for about 45 minutes until the potatoes are tender.

AFRICAN CURRIED VEGETABLES

Metric/imperial		American
1 × 15ml spoon/ 1 tablespoon	cooking oil	1 tablespoon
	1 onion, sliced	
1 × 5ml spoon/ 1 teaspoon	curry powder	1 teaspoon
1 × 5ml spoon/ 1 teaspoon	cumin	1 teaspoon
1 × 5ml spoon/ 1 teaspoon	dried coriander	1 teaspoon
$\frac{1}{2}$ × 2.5ml spoon/ $\frac{1}{4}$ teaspoon	ground ginger	$\frac{1}{4}$ teaspoon
	2 cloves	
	4 cardamoms	
450g/1 lb	mixed vegetables, chopped (see **Note**)	1 lb
600ml/1 pint	water	2½ cups
1 × 15ml spoon/ 1 tablespoon	peanut butter	1 tablespoon
	salt, freshly ground pepper	

Heat the oil in a pan, and cook the onion with the spices until lightly browned. Add the vegetables and the water, heat to boiling point, then simmer for about 30–40 minutes. Drain well, then mix the liquid with the peanut butter. Return to the pan, and season to taste. Simmer for a further 5–10 minutes before serving.

Note Use cauliflower, carrots and potatoes.

SESAME POTATO PATTIES

Metric/imperial		American
675g/1½ lb	potatoes, peeled	1½ lb
50g/2 oz	butter **or** margarine	4 tablespoons
350g/12 oz	ground cooked soya beans	1½ cups
2 × 15ml spoons/ 2 tablespoons	toasted ground sesame seeds	3 tablespoons
	salt, freshly ground pepper	
2 × 15ml spoons/ 2 tablespoons	wholemeal flour, sifted	3 tablespoons
2–3 × 15ml spoons/ 2–3 tablespoons	cooking oil	3–4 tablespoons

Boil the potatoes until soft, then drain and mash with butter. Add the soya beans, sesame seeds and the salt and pepper, and mix well. Shape into patties, coat with the flour, and fry in cooking oil until brown on both sides.
  Serve with Banana Sauce (page 68).

Sesame Potato Patties with Banana Sauce (page 68)

SPINACH LASAGNE WITH TOMATO SAUCE

Metric/imperial		American
	8 sheets wholemeal (wholewheat) lasagne	
1 × 15ml spoon/ 1 tablespoon	olive oil	1 tablespoon
	salt, freshly ground pepper	
900g/2 lb	fresh leaf spinach	2 lb
15g/½ oz	butter **or** margarine	1 tablespoon
350g/12 oz	cottage cheese	1½ cups
1 × 5ml spoon/ 1 teaspoon	celery seed **or** celery salt	1 teaspoon
1 × 15ml spoon/ 1 tablespoon	cooking oil	1 tablespoon
	1 onion, finely chopped	
450g/1 lb	tomatoes, skinned and chopped	1 lb
2 × 15ml spoon/ 2 tablespoons	concentrated tomato purée (paste)	3 tablespoons
1 × 5ml spoon/ 1 teaspoon	dried oregano	1 teaspoon
	Parmesan cheese, grated	

Cook the lasagne in a large pan of steadily boiling water until *al dente* with the oil and salt, then drain.

Meanwhile, cook the spinach with a little butter until soft, then drain.

Spread each sheet of lasagne with cottage cheese, spinach and the celery seed or salt. Roll up, then place in a casserole.

Heat the oil in a pan, and cook the onion until soft. Add the tomatoes, tomato purée (paste), oregano and salt and pepper to taste, then simmer until the vegetables are cooked through. Pass through a sieve or process in a blender or food processor.

Pour the tomato sauce over the lasagne, sprinkle with a little Parmesan cheese, and cook in a fairly hot oven, 200°C/400°F/Gas 6, for about 15 minutes until browned.

MEXICAN BAKED SPINACH

Metric/imperial		American
900g/2 lb	fresh leaf spinach	2 lb
	1 large green pepper, de-seeded and sliced	
1 × 15ml spoon/ 1 tablespoon	cooking oil	1 tablespoon
	1 onion, finely chopped	
	$\frac{1}{4}$ head celery, finely chopped	
$\frac{1}{2}$ × 2.5ml spoon/ $\frac{1}{4}$ teaspoon	ground cinnamon	$\frac{1}{4}$ teaspoon
	a pinch of Cayenne pepper	
	a pinch of dill seed	
75g/3 oz	hard cheese, grated	$\frac{3}{4}$ cup
3 × 15ml spoon/ 3 tablespoons	tomato juice	4 tablespoons
	salt, freshly ground pepper	

Steam the spinach in a large pan for 5 minutes until considerably reduced with just the water that clings to the leaves. Blanch the pepper for 5 minutes in boiling water. Heat the oil in a pan, and cook the onion and celery for 5 minutes with the cinnamon, Cayenne pepper and the dill seed.

Place half the spinach in the base of an oval earthenware dish, add a layer of pepper, then all the onion and celery mixture. Sprinkle with half the cheese, and cover with the remaining pepper. Add the remaining spinach, pour on the tomato juice, and top with the remaining cheese. Sprinkle each layer with salt and pepper as you go. Bake in a fairly hot oven, 190°C/375°F/Gas 5, for 45 minutes until browned.

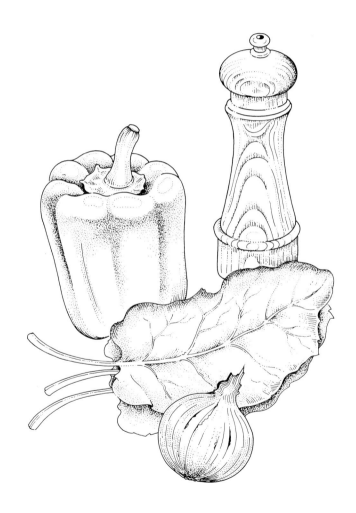

43

CAULIFLOWER MACARONI

Metric/imperial		American
225g/8 oz	wholemeal (wholewheat) macaroni	½ lb
1 × 15ml spoon/ 1 tablespoon	olive oil	1 tablespoon
	salt, freshly ground pepper	
	1 cauliflower, broken into florets	
25g/1 oz	butter **or** margarine	2 tablespoons
25g/1 oz	wholemeal (wholewheat) flour, sifted	¼ cup
600ml/1 pint	milk	2½ cups
100g/4 oz	hard cheese, grated	1 cup
	2 tomatoes, sliced	
50g/2 oz	wholemeal (wholewheat) breadcrumbs	1 cup

Cook the macaroni in a large pan of steadily boiling water until *al dente* with the olive oil and salt. Cook the cauliflower in a pan of boiling salted water until tender.

Meanwhile, melt the fat in a pan, stir in the flour over low heat, then add the milk, and cook until the sauce thickens, stirring all the time. Add most of the cheese, then season to taste.

Place the macaroni and cauliflower in a casserole, and cover with the cheese sauce. Lay the sliced tomatoes on top, then sprinkle with the reserved cheese and the breadcrumbs. Brown under a hot grill (broiler).

PASTA WITH PEANUT SAUCE

Metric/imperial		American
350g/12 oz	wholemeal (wholewheat) pasta	¾ lb
1 × 15ml spoon/ 1 tablespoon	olive oil	1 tablespoon
	salt	
	SAUCE	
15g/½ oz	butter	1 tablespoon
	1 small onion, grated	
	1 carrot, grated	
2 × 15ml spoons/ 2 tablespoons	peanut butter	3 tablespoons
150ml/¼ pint	milk	⅔ cup
2 × 15ml spoons/ 2 tablespoons	lemon juice	3 tablespoons

Cook the pasta in a large pan of steadily boiling water until *al dente* with the olive oil and salt, then drain.

To make the sauce, melt the butter in a pan and cook the onion and carrot until soft. Add the peanut butter, then stir in the milk and lemon juice. Add enough water to give a smooth creamy consistency. Heat to boiling point, then simmer for 5 minutes, adding more water if necessary.

Drain the pasta, and serve with the peanut sauce poured over the top.

POLENTA TOMATO CASSEROLE

Metric/imperial		American
900ml/1½ pints	water	3¾ cups
100g/4 oz	yellow cornmeal	generous ¾ cup
1 × 2.5ml spoon/ ½ teaspoon	salt	½ teaspoon
100g/4 oz	butter **or** margarine	½ cup
100g/4 oz	Parmesan cheese, grated	1 cup
½ × 2.5ml spoon/ ¼ teaspoon (approx)	ground nutmeg	¼ teaspoon (approx)
50g/2 oz	wholemeal flour, sifted	½ cup
400ml/⅔ pint	milk	1¾ cups
	3 onions, finely sliced	
	4 large tomatoes, skinned and thinly sliced	
25g/1 oz	wholemeal (wholewheat) breadcrumbs	½ cup

Heat the water to boiling point, then pour in the cornmeal, stirring all the time. Add the salt and 50g/2 oz/¼ US cup butter, and continue stirring until the mixture thickens. Cook on low heat for 20–30 minutes, stirring all the time. The finished mixture should be thick and smooth. Add 50g/2 oz/½ US cup Parmesan cheese and the nutmeg, and season to taste. Pour into a basin and leave to cool and set.

Meanwhile, melt the remaining butter in a pan, stir in the flour over low heat, then add the milk, and cook until the sauce thickens, stirring all the time. Season to taste.

Slice the cold polenta into thin wedges, and layer in a casserole with the sliced onions and tomatoes. Sprinkle with the remaining cheese, and top with the sauce. Top with the breadcrumbs and a little more nutmeg. Bake in a fairly hot oven, 190°C/375°F/Gas 5, for 30–40 minutes until browned.

Cottage Cheese Pancakes with Avocado Sauce

Metric/imperial		American
	1 egg	
900ml/1½ pints	milk	3¾ cups
175g/6 oz	wholemeal (wholewheat) flour, sifted	1½ cups
	salt, freshly ground pepper	
450g/1 lb	cottage cheese	2 cups
50g/2 oz	butter **or** margarine	4 tablespoons
	3 ripe avocado pears, peeled, stoned (pitted) and sliced	
	GARNISH sprigs watercress	

Beat the egg with a little milk, then add 100g/4 oz/1 US cup flour and salt. Mix to a stiff batter, and beat well. Add 300ml/½ pint/1¼ US cups milk, and leave for 1 hour.

Make eight pancakes with the batter, and spread each one with cottage cheese mixed with salt and pepper. Roll up and place in an ovenproof dish.

Melt the butter in a pan, stir in the remaining flour over low heat, then add the remaining milk, and cook until the sauce thickens, stirring all the time. Sieve the avocado pears into the sauce, season to taste, and pour over the pancakes. Cook in a moderate oven, 180°C/350°F/Gas 4, for 30 minutes until heated through. Garnish with sprigs of watercress before serving.

Oat, Cheese and Tomato Flan

Metric/imperial		American
50g/2 oz	butter **or** margarine	4 tablespoons
50g/2 oz	wholemeal (wholewheat) flour, sifted	½ cup
50g/2 oz	rolled oats	½ cup
	salt, freshly ground pepper	
1 × 15ml spoon/ 1 tablespoon	cooking oil	1 tablespoon
	2 large onions, finely chopped	
50g/2 oz	ground hazelnuts (filberts)	½ cup
100g/4 oz	Edam cheese, grated	1 cup
2 × 15ml spoons/ 2 tablespoons	concentrated tomato purée (paste)	3 tablespoons
	1½ eggs, beaten	
1½ × 15ml spoons/ 1½ tablespoons	double (heavy) cream	2 tablespoons

Rub (cut in) the fat into the flour, oats and salt, and bind with a little water. Press into one 20cm/8 inch flan case (pie pan).

Heat the oil in a pan, and cook the onions until transparent. Mix with the remaining ingredients.

Place the mixture in the pastry case (pie shell), and bake in a fairly hot oven, 200°C/400°F/Gas 6, for about 45 minutes until browned. Leave to cool before serving.

LANCASHIRE CHEESE LOG

Metric/imperial		American
225g/8 oz	Lancashire cheese, grated	2 cups
	2 small gherkins, finely chopped	
	3 stuffed olives, finely chopped	
1 × 5ml spoon/ 1 teaspoon	fresh chives, chopped	1 teaspoon
$\frac{1}{2}$ × 2.5ml spoon/ $\frac{1}{4}$ teaspoon	dried thyme	$\frac{1}{4}$ teaspoon
$\frac{1}{2}$ × 2.5ml spoon/ $\frac{1}{4}$ teaspoon	French (Dijon-style) mustard	$\frac{1}{4}$ teaspoon
	salt, freshly ground black pepper	
2 × 15ml spoons/ 2 tablespoons	mayonnaise	3 tablespoons
	lettuce leaves	

Mix together the cheese, gherkins, olives, chives, herbs, mustard and seasoning. Bind with mayonnaise to make a stiffish mixture, then shape into a roll, and wrap in grease-proof (waxed) paper. Chill for 1 hour, and serve sliced on a bed of lettuce.

SLICED PEANUT LOAF

Metric/imperial		American
100g/4 oz	mushrooms, finely chopped	1 cup
	3 onions, finely chopped	
	2 tomatoes, finely chopped	
2 × 15ml spoons/ 2 tablespoons	peanut butter	3 tablespoons
50g/2 oz	ground peanuts	$\frac{1}{2}$ cup
50g/2 oz	soya flour	$\frac{1}{2}$ cup
50g/2 oz	wholemeal (wholewheat) breadcrumbs	1 cup
	2 eggs	
2 × 5ml spoons/ 2 teaspoons	dill seed	2 teaspoons
	salt, freshly ground pepper	
25g/1 oz	medium oatmeal	2 tablespoons

Mix together all the ingredients except the oatmeal. Form into a loaf shape, and roll in the oatmeal. Place on a greased baking sheet, then bake in a moderate oven, 180°C/350°F/Gas 4, for 45 minutes–1 hour until crisp. Leave to cool, then serve sliced.

WHITBOURNE SURPRISE EGGS

Metric/imperial		American
	4 hard-boiled (hard-cooked) eggs, halved	
1 × 5ml spoon/ 1 teaspoon	mayonnaise	1 teaspoon
1 × 2.5ml spoon/ ½ teaspoon	dried mixed herbs	½ teaspoon
1 × 15ml spoon/ 1 tablespoon	agar-agar	1 tablespoon
600ml/1 pint	boiling water	2½ cups
1 × 5ml spoon/ 1 teaspoon	yeast (vegetable) extract	1 teaspoon
	1 large gherkin, chopped	

Separate the yolks from the eggs, and mix with the mayonnaise and herbs. Pile the mixture back into the egg whites, and push the two halves together.

Sprinkle the agar-agar into the boiling water, add the yeast (vegetable) extract, and stir until completely dissolved.

Place the stuffed eggs in small moulds, and surround with the chopped gherkin. Pour over the agar-agar mixture, and leave to set in a cool place.

'SCOTCH' EGGS

Metric/imperial		American
50g/2 oz	butter **or** margarine	4 tablespoons
50g/2 oz	wholemeal (wholewheat) flour	½ cup
350ml/12 fl oz	milk	1½ cups
50g/2 oz	buckwheat flour	½ cup
100g/4 oz	ground peanuts	1 cup
	salt, freshly ground pepper	
	4 hard-boiled (hard-cooked) eggs	
	1 egg, beaten	
100g/4 oz	dried wholemeal (wholewheat) breadcrumbs	1 cup

Melt the butter in a pan, stir in the flour over low heat, then add the milk, and cook until the sauce thickens, stirring all the time. Add the buckwheat flour, and cook for a further 5 minutes. Add the ground peanuts and salt and pepper to taste, then leave to cool.

Divide the cooled mixture into four portions, and shape each round one hard-boiled (hard-cooked) egg. Dip in the beaten egg, and coat well with breadcrumbs. Deep fry until golden-brown.

'Scotch' Eggs **and** *Rocky Mountain Salad (page 51)*

Hazelnut Terrine en Croûte

Metric/imperial		American
	2 onions, chopped	
	3 sticks celery, chopped	
	½ green pepper, de-seeded and chopped	
75g/3 oz	ground hazelnuts (filberts)	¾ cup
100g/4 oz	wholemeal (wholewheat) breadcrumbs	2 cups
1 × 5ml spoon/ 1 teaspoon	dried marjoram	1 teaspoon
1 × 2.5ml spoon/ ½ teaspoon	ground cumin seed	½ teaspoon
1 × 5ml spoon/ 1 teaspoon	freshly chopped sage	1 teaspoon
	salt, freshly ground pepper	
	4 eggs, beaten	
75g/3 oz	butter **or** margarine	6 tablespoons
225g/8 oz	wholemeal (wholewheat) flour, sifted	2 cups

Mix together the onions, celery and pepper, and mix with the nuts, breadcrumbs, herbs and seasoning. Bind with two beaten eggs.

To make the pastry, rub (cut in) the butter into the flour and salt, and bind with one egg. Roll out three-quarters of the pastry on a lightly floured surface, and place the terrine mixture in the centre of the pastry. Wrap the pastry round the mixture, sealing the top and sides. Roll out the remaining pastry, and cut out leaf shapes, then arrange them on top of the roll to mask the join. Press down with a little water on the joined surfaces, and brush with the remaining beaten egg. Bake in a fairly hot oven, 200°C/400°F/Gas 6, for 45–50 minutes until the pastry is crisp and lightly browned. Cool on a wire rack.

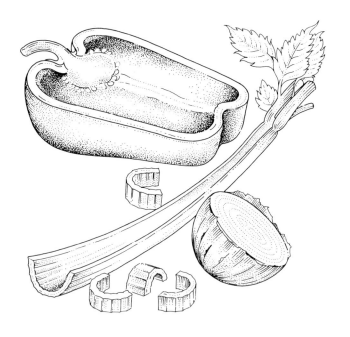

ROCKY MOUNTAIN SALAD

Metric/imperial		American
175g/6 oz	brown rice	scant 1 cup
	salt, pepper	
	3 hard-boiled (hard-cooked) eggs, finely chopped	
	3 large gherkins, finely chopped	
	1 small green pepper, de-seeded and finely chopped	
1 × 5ml spoon/ 1 teaspoon	dried rosemary	1 teaspoon
1 × 15ml spoon/ 1 tablespoon	mayonnaise	1 tablespoon
225g/8 oz	cooked red kidney beans	1⅓ cups
100g/4 oz	cooked broad (fava or lima) beans	¾ cup
50g/2 oz	cooked haricot (navy) **or** black-eyed beans	⅓ cup
	1 small onion, finely chopped	
1 × 15ml spoon/ 1 tablespoon	fresh parsley, finely chopped	1 tablespoon
4 × 15ml spoons/ 4 tablespoons	French dressing	5 tablespoons

Cook the rice in boiling salted water, then drain and leave to cool.

Mix the rice with the eggs, gherkins, pepper, rosemary and salt and pepper, then bind with the mayonnaise. Pack into a greased 900ml/1½ pint/3¾ US cup pudding basin (heatproof mixing bowl), and chill for 1 hour.

Meanwhile, mix together the beans, onion and parsley, and toss in the dressing.

Turn out the rice mixture on to a serving dish, and surround with the bean salad.

GREEK SALAD

Metric/imperial		American
	½ lettuce, coarsely chopped	
	4 tomatoes, coarsely chopped	
	10cm/4 inch length cucumber, coarsely chopped	
	sprigs watercress	
	8 radishes	
	8 spring onions (scallions)	
	12 black (ripe) olives	
4 × 15ml spoons/ 4 tablespoons	olive oil	5 tablespoons
1–2 × 15ml spoons/ 1–2 tablespoons	vinegar	1–3 tablespoons
1 × 5ml spoon/ 1 teaspoon	dried thyme	1 teaspoon
1 × 2.5ml spoon/ ½ teaspoon	dried oregano	½ teaspoon
	black pepper	
225g/8 oz	Feta cheese, flaked	2 cups

Arrange the vegetables in a bowl. Mix together the oil and vinegar with the herbs and pepper, and pour this over the salad. Top with the Feta cheese.
 Serve with hot pitta bread.

EGG AND ALMOND SALAD

Metric/imperial		American
	6 hard-boiled (hard-cooked) eggs, diced	
2 × 15ml spoons/ 2 tablespoons	flaked (slivered) almonds, chopped	3 tablespoons
50g/2 oz	Cheshire cheese, diced	½ cup
	4 cooked beetroot (beet), diced	
	½ cucumber, diced	
	4 spring onions (scallions), chopped	
50g/2 oz	mushrooms, chopped	½ cup
	salt, freshly ground pepper	
4 × 15ml spoons/ 4 tablespoons	mayonnaise	5 tablespoons

GARNISH
4 tomatoes, sliced

chopped parsley

Mix together the eggs, almonds, cheese, beetroot (beet), cucumber, spring onions (scallions) and mushrooms with the seasoning and mayonnaise. Pile on to a serving dish, and surround with sliced tomato. Sprinkle with chopped parsley.

Greek Salad

Napoleon Rice Cake

Metric/imperial		American
175g/6 oz	brown rice	scant 1 cup
175g/6 oz	fresh peas	1 cup
75g/3 oz	walnuts, chopped	$\frac{3}{4}$ cup
75g/3 oz	almonds, chopped	$\frac{3}{4}$ cup
	1 onion, chopped	
1 × 5ml spoon/ 1 teaspoon	dried thyme	1 teaspoon
1 × 15ml spoon/ 1 tablespoon	French dressing	1 tablespoon
	salt, freshly ground pepper	
	GARNISH sliced beetroot (beet), cooked	

Cook the rice and peas separately, in boiling salted water until tender. Drain, then leave to cool.

Mix together the nuts, onion, rice and peas, then add the herbs, dressing and seasoning to taste. Press into a 900ml/1½ pint/3¾ US cup greased pudding basin (heatproof mixing bowl), then chill for 1 hour.

Carefully turn out on to a serving dish, and re-shape if necessary. Garnish with sliced beetroot (beet) just before serving.

Tomato and Oregano Cheesecake

Metric/imperial		American
	10 unsweetened wheatmeal biscuits (wholewheat cookies), crushed	
40g/1½ oz	butter **or** margarine, melted	3 tablespoons
225g/8 oz	cottage cheese	1 cup
450g/1 lb	canned tomatoes	1 lb
2 × 5ml spoons/ 2 teaspoons	gelozone (vegetarian setting agent)	2 teaspoons
4 × 15ml spoons/ 4 tablespoons	water	5 tablespoons
	salt, freshly ground pepper	
1 × 5ml spoon/ 1 teaspoon	dried oregano	1 teaspoon

Mix together the biscuits (cookies) and melted butter, then press into the base of a loose-bottomed 17.5cm/7 inch cake tin (spring-form pan). Bake in a very cool oven, 140°C/275°F/Gas 1, for 8 minutes, then remove from the oven, and leave to cool.

Meanwhile, pass the cottage cheese and canned tomatoes through a sieve or process in a blender or food processor. Blend the gelozone (setting agent) and water to form a paste, then heat to boiling point, and simmer for 2–3 minutes. Mix together with the cottage cheese and tomatoes, then season to taste and mix in the oregano.

Pour the cheese mixture into the cold base, and chill until set. Remove from the tin (pan) before serving.

SIDE ATTRACTIONS

SAVOY PEAS

Metric/imperial		American
	2 leeks, sliced	
225g/8 oz	fresh peas	1½ cups
	1 clove of garlic, crushed	
	salt, freshly ground pepper	
	vegetable stock	

Arrange the leeks in a casserole with the peas. Add the garlic, salt and pepper and enough vegetable stock to come about one-third of the way up the vegetables. Cover, and cook in a hot oven, 220°C/425°F/Gas 7, for about 45 minutes until the vegetables are tender.

CAULIFLOWER AMANDINE

Metric/imperial		American
	1 cauliflower	
15g/½ oz	butter **or** margarine	1 tablespoon
15g/½ oz	wholemeal (wholewheat) flour, sifted	2 tablespoons
250ml/8 fl oz	milk	1 cup
	salt, freshly ground pepper	
25g/1 oz	flaked (slivered) almonds	¼ cup
25g/1 oz	toasted wholemeal (wholewheat) breadcrumbs	¼ cup

Steam the cauliflower until cooked, then turn into a serving dish with the florets upwards.

Melt the butter in a pan, stir in the flour over low heat, then add the milk, and cook until the sauce thickens, stirring all the time. Season to taste, then add the almonds, retaining a few.

Pour the sauce over the cauliflower, and sprinkle with the toasted breadcrumbs and the reserved almonds.

Devonshire Carrots and Turnips

Metric/imperial		American
1 × 5ml spoon/ 1 teaspoon	honey	1 teaspoon
3 × 15ml spoons/ 3 tablespoons	dry (hard) cider	4 tablespoons
225g/8 oz	carrots, coarsely chopped	1⅓ cups
225g/8 oz	turnips, coarsely chopped	1⅓ cups
	salt, freshly ground pepper	

Dissolve the honey in the cider. Put the carrots and turnips in a casserole, and pour over the sweetened cider. Season to taste, then cover and cook in a fairly hot oven, 200°C/400°F/Gas 6, for 1 hour until the vegetables are tender.

Almond Carrots

Metric/imperial		American
450g/1 lb	carrots, grated	1 lb
	salt, freshly ground pepper	
	a little vegetable stock	
50g/2 oz	flaked (slivered) almonds	½ cup
½ × 2.5ml spoon/ ¼ teaspoon	dried basil	¼ teaspoon
15g/½ oz	butter	1 tablespoon

Cook the carrots in a little seasoned vegetable stock, then drain and mix with the almonds and basil. Dot with flakes of butter, and serve at once.

Orange Beetroot

Metric/imperial		American
15g/½ oz	butter **or** margarine	1 tablespoon
450g/1 lb	cooked beetroot (beet), diced	1 lb
	grated rind of ½ orange	
1 × 15ml spoon/ 1 tablespoon	orange juice	1 tablespoon
	black pepper	

Melt the butter in a pan and heat the beetroot (beet). Add the orange rind and juice, then heat through again but do not boil. Sprinkle with black pepper, and serve at once.

Aubergine Corn

Metric/imperial		American
1 × 15ml spoon/ 1 tablespoon	cooking oil	1 tablespoon
	2 medium aubergines (eggplants), sliced	
	2 corn-on-the-cob (ears of corn), stripped from the cob	
175g/6 oz	tomatoes, skinned and sliced	$\frac{3}{4}$ cup
	salt, freshly ground pepper	
25g/1 oz	wholemeal (wholewheat) breadcrumbs	$\frac{1}{2}$ cup
15g/$\frac{1}{2}$ oz	butter **or** margarine	1 tablespoon

Heat the oil in a pan, and cook the sliced aubergines (eggplants) until soft. Layer in a casserole with the corn and tomatoes, seasoning each layer. Sprinkle with the breadcrumbs, and dot with flakes of butter. Bake in a fairly hot oven, 190°C/375°F/Gas 5, for 45 minutes until lightly browned.

Nut Dumplings

Metric/imperial		American
25g/1 oz	wholemeal (wholewheat) breadcrumbs	$\frac{1}{2}$ cup
2 × 15ml spoons/ 2 tablespoons	milk	3 tablespoons
25g/1 oz	ground peanuts	$\frac{1}{4}$ cup
	1 egg, beaten	
	a little 81% extraction self-raising flour	
	salt, freshly ground pepper	

Soak the breadcrumbs in the milk. Add the peanuts and egg, and beat well. If the mixture is too liquid to form into balls, add some flour to make a stiffish paste. Season to taste, then shape into 20 small dumplings about 1.25cm/ $\frac{1}{2}$ inch in diameter. Drop into soup or into boiling salted water, and cook for 5–8 minutes.

SPINACH MOUNTAIN

Metric/imperial		American
900g/2 lb	fresh leaf spinach	2 lb
2 × 5ml spoons/ 2 teaspoons	raisins	2 teaspoons
	ground nutmeg	
	salt, freshly ground pepper	
3–4 × 15ml spoons/ 3–4 tablespoons	double (heavy) cream	4–5 tablespoons

Cook the spinach in a large pan for about 6–8 minutes until tender with just the water that clings to the leaves, then chop finely. Mix in the raisins, nutmeg and seasoning, then pile on to a serving plate, and pour the cream over the top. Serve at once.

POTATO CAKES

Metric/imperial		American
450g/1 lb	potatoes, peeled	1 lb
50g/2 oz	butter **or** margarine	4 tablespoons
3 × 15ml spoons/ 3 tablespoons	vegetable stock	4 tablespoons
4 × 15ml spoons/ 4 tablespoons	wholemeal (wholewheat) flour	5 tablespoons
	salt, freshly ground pepper	

Boil the potatoes until soft, then mash with the butter and stock, and mix in the flour and salt and pepper to taste. Press out on a greased baking sheet to about 6mm/¼ inch thickness, and mark into sections with a knife. Bake in a fairly hot oven, 200°C/400°F/Gas 6, for 40–45 minutes until slightly crisp and brown.

Serve with butter or margarine.

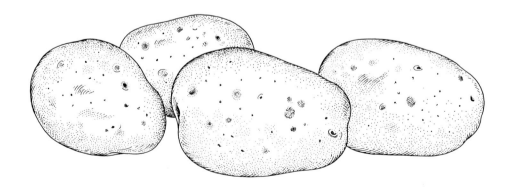

SPANISH LENTILS

Metric/imperial		American
100g/4 oz	lentils	½ cup
¾ × 5ml spoon/ ¾ teaspoon	yeast (vegetable) extract	¾ teaspoon
600ml/1 pint	water	2½ cups
	1 small onion, finely chopped	
	1 tomato, finely chopped	
	¼ green pepper	
1 × 5ml spoon/ 1 teaspoon	dried marjoram	1 teaspoon
	salt, freshly ground pepper	

Cook the lentils with the yeast (vegetable) extract and water for 30 minutes, then add the vegetables, marjoram and seasoning. Simmer for a further hour or until all the vegetables are cooked and the mixture is fairly thick.

DAHL

Metric/imperial		American
100g/4 oz	lentils	½ cup
600ml/1 pint	water	2½ cups
1 × 2.5ml spoon/ ½ teaspoon	turmeric	½ teaspoon
	salt	
1 × 15ml spoon/ 1 tablespoon	cooking oil	1 tablespoon
	1 small onion, sliced	
	1 clove of garlic (optional)	
	1 piece of stem ginger	

Cook the lentils with the water for 45 minutes. Add the turmeric and salt, and cook for about 30 minutes until the lentils are really soft.

Meanwhile, heat the oil in a separate pan, and cook the onion, garlic, if used, and the ginger until lightly browned. Add to the lentils just before serving.

JOLLOF RICE

Metric/imperial		American
1 × 15ml spoon/ 1 tablespoon	cooking oil	1 tablespoon
	1 onion, finely chopped	
100g/4 oz	long-grain brown rice	$\frac{2}{3}$ cup
15g/$\frac{1}{2}$ oz	raisins	1 tablespoon
225g/8 oz	canned tomatoes	1 cup
	Cayenne pepper	
	salt	
150ml/$\frac{1}{4}$ pint	vegetable stock	$\frac{2}{3}$ cup
25g/1 oz	roasted peanuts	$\frac{1}{4}$ cup

Heat the oil in a pan, and cook the onion until soft and beginning to brown. Add the rice, and cook gently for a further 3–4 minutes, stirring occasionally. Stir in the dried fruit, tomatoes, seasoning and stock, then cook for about 30 minutes until the rice is tender and the liquid just absorbed. Add the peanuts, and cook for a further 5 minutes, stirring occasionally.

BAKED VEGETABLE RICE

Metric/imperial		American
50g/2 oz	cooked brown rice	scant $\frac{1}{2}$ cup
100g/4 oz	cooked new potatoes, diced	$\frac{2}{3}$ cup
225g/8 oz	marrow (squash), diced	1$\frac{1}{3}$ cups
50g/2 oz	red pepper, de-seeded and diced	$\frac{1}{2}$ cup
25g/1 oz	hard cheese, grated	$\frac{1}{4}$ cup
15g/$\frac{1}{2}$ oz	butter **or** margarine	1 tablespoon
	salt, freshly ground pepper	

Mix together all the ingredients, and place in a casserole. Dot with flakes of butter or margarine, and cook in a moderate oven, 180°C/350°F/Gas 4, for 1 hour.

Avocado Risotto (page 38) **and** *Jollof Rice*

GREEN POTATO SALAD

Metric/imperial		American
350g/12 oz	potatoes	¾ lb
	1 head of chicory (endive), chopped	
	1 small bunch of chives, chopped	
	watercress, chopped	
	4–6 Cos (romaine) lettuce leaves, chopped	
	DRESSING	
6 × 15ml spoons/ 6 tablespoons	salad oil	7 tablespoons
3 × 15ml spoons/ 3 tablespoons	wine vinegar	4 tablespoons
1 × 5ml spoon/ 1 teaspoon	French (Dijon-style) mustard	1 teaspoon
	salt, freshly ground black pepper	

Boil the potatoes, then dice while still hot.

To make the dressing, mix together the oil, vinegar, mustard and seasoning, and pour this over the warm potatoes. Leave to cool, then add the chicory (endive), chives, watercress and lettuce leaves just before serving.

SPROUT AND CELERY SALAD

Metric/imperial		American
175g/6 oz	Brussels sprouts, finely chopped	scant 2 cups
	½ head celery, finely chopped	
100g/4 oz	mushrooms, finely chopped	1 cup
3 × 15ml spoons/ 3 tablespoons	cashew nuts	4 tablespoons
3 × 15ml spoons/ 3 tablespoons	raisins	4 tablespoons
	dried marjoram	
	salt, freshly ground pepper	
4 × 15ml spoons/ 4 tablespoons	French dressing	5 tablespoons

Mix the vegetables with the nuts and raisins, then add the marjoram, salt, pepper and the dressing. Toss well, then serve.

BEANSHOOT AND ONION SALAD

Metric/imperial		American
350g/12 oz	beanshoots	6 cups
	1 bunch spring onions (scallions), sliced lengthways	
	½ green pepper, de-seeded and finely sliced	
3 × 15ml spoons/ 3 tablespoons	French dressing	4 tablespoons
	black pepper	

Toss the vegetables in the dressing, then sprinkle with black pepper.

RAW FENNEL SALAD

Metric/imperial		American
	1 medium fennel heart, chopped	
	8 radishes, finely chopped	
	4 spring onions (scallions), finely chopped	
	2 sticks celery, finely chopped	
2 × 15ml spoons/ 2 tablespoons	French dressing	3 tablespoons
1 × 2.5ml spoon/ ½ teaspoon	dried marjoram	½ teaspoon
	black pepper	

Mix together the fennel, radishes, spring onions (scallions) and celery with the dressing, marjoram and black pepper. Serve at once.

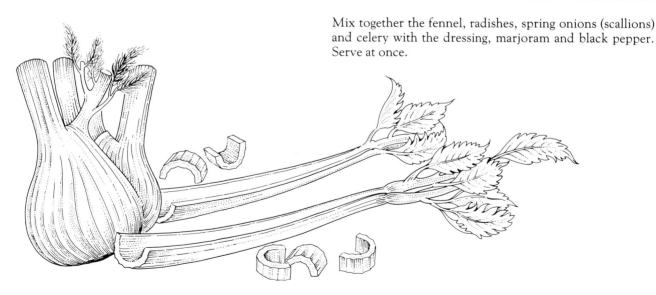

Orange Banana Salad

Metric/imperial		American
2 × 15ml spoons/ 2 tablespoons	smooth peanut butter	3 tablespoons
1 × 5ml spoon/ 1 teaspoon	grated orange rind	1 teaspoon
25g/1 oz	crystallized ginger, finely chopped (optional)	¼ cup
	2 bananas, split lengthways	
2 × 15ml spoons/ 2 tablespoons	mayonnaise	3 tablespoons
½ × 15ml spoon/ ½ tablespoon	orange juice	½ tablespoon
50g/2 oz	roasted peanuts, chopped	½ cup
	endive	
	GARNISH orange slices	

Mix together the peanut butter, orange rind and the ginger, if used, then spread on to one-half of each banana, and top with the other half. Cut each into four pieces. Mix the mayonnaise with the orange juice, then dip each banana piece into this, and roll in the peanuts until coated on all sides. Serve on a bed of endive, and garnish with orange slices.

Carrot and Orange Salad

chopped segments of 1 orange
juice of 1 orange
2 large carrots, coarsely grated
black pepper
GARNISH 4 black (ripe) olives

Mix together the chopped orange segments and the juice with the carrots, then season well with black pepper. Garnish with black (ripe) olives.

Orange Banana Salad

MIXED BEAN SALAD

Metric/imperial		American
25g/1 oz	haricot (navy) beans	1½ tablespoons
25g/1 oz	black eye beans	1½ tablespoons
25g/1 oz	soya beans	1½ tablespoons
25g/1 oz	red kidney beans	1½ tablespoons
	4 spring onions (scallions), finely chopped	
4 × 15ml spoons/ 4 tablespoons	French dressing	5 tablespoons
	salt, freshly ground black pepper	

Soak the beans overnight in cold water, then drain, discarding the water. Boil briskly in fresh water for at least 10 minutes, then cook for about 1–2 hours until soft. Mix together with the spring onions (scallions), pour over the dressing, and season to taste with salt and black pepper. Leave to cool.

SAVOURY RICE

Metric/imperial		American
75g/3 oz	brown rice	scant ½ cup
	salt, freshly ground pepper	
100g/4 oz	mushrooms, finely chopped	1 cup
	½ green pepper, de-seeded and finely chopped	
225g/8 oz	sweetcorn kernels	1½ cups
1 × 15ml spoon/ 1 tablespoon	salad oil	1 tablespoon
1 × 15ml spoon/ 1 tablespoon	vinegar	1 tablespoon
1 × 2.5ml spoon/ ½ teaspoon	dried thyme	½ teaspoon
1 × 2.5ml spoon/ ½ teaspoon	celery seed **or** celery salt	½ teaspoon

Cook the rice in salted water, then drain well. Leave to cool. Add the mushrooms, pepper and sweetcorn. Mix together the oil, vinegar, herbs and seasoning, then toss the vegetables in the dressing.

PASTA NUT SALAD

Metric/imperial		American
100g/4 oz	wholemeal (wholewheat) pasta shapes	1 cup
1 × 15ml spoon/ 1 tablespoon	olive oil	1 tablespoon
	salt	
	1 shallot, finely chopped	
	1 green pepper, finely chopped	
50g/2 oz	roasted peanuts	$\frac{1}{2}$ cup
65g/2$\frac{1}{2}$ oz	flaked (slivered) almonds	generous $\frac{1}{2}$ cup
65g/2$\frac{1}{2}$oz	raisins	generous $\frac{1}{3}$ cup
150ml/$\frac{1}{4}$ pint	yoghurt	$\frac{2}{3}$ cup
1 × 15ml spoon/ 1 tablespoon	lemon juice	1 tablespoon

Cook the pasta in a large pan of steadily boiling water until *al dente* with the olive oil and salt. Drain, then leave to cool.

Mix the cooked pasta with the shallot and pepper, then add most of the nuts and raisins, the yoghurt and lemon juice, and mix well. Garnish with the remaining nuts and raisins.

MEXICAN SAUCE

Metric/imperial		American
1 × 15ml spoon/ 1 tablespoon	cooking oil	1 tablespoon
	1 red pepper, de-seeded and finely chopped	
	1 green pepper, de-seeded and finely chopped	
	1 clove of garlic, finely chopped	
	8 tomatoes, chopped	
1 × 5ml spoon/ 1 teaspoon	dried coriander	1 teaspoon
	2 cloves	
1 × 2.5ml spoon/ $\frac{1}{2}$ teaspoon	chilli powder	$\frac{1}{2}$ teaspoon
300ml/$\frac{1}{2}$ pint	vegetable stock	1$\frac{1}{4}$ cups
	salt, freshly ground pepper	

Heat the oil in a pan and cook the peppers and garlic for 5 minutes. Add the tomatoes and the remaining ingredients, then heat to boiling point. Simmer for 20 minutes, then pass through a sieve or process in a blender or food processor. Season to taste.

Banana Sauce

Metric/imperial		American
	2 bananas	
	juice of 1 lemon	
1 × 15ml spoon/ 1 tablespoon	cooking oil	1 tablespoon
	1 onion, finely chopped	
	1 small green pepper, de-seeded and finely chopped	
	salt, freshly ground pepper	
2 × 15ml spoons/ 2 tablespoons	fresh mint, chopped	3 tablespoons
2 × 15ml spoons/ 2 tablespoons	fresh parsley, chopped	3 tablespoons

Mash the bananas, then mix with the lemon juice; add a little water if necessary to give a creamy consistency. Heat the oil in a pan, and cook the onion and pepper, then add the seasoning, herbs and the banana mixture. Simmer for 20 minutes, then pass through a sieve or process in a blender or food processor. Serve at once.

Banana Sambal

Metric/imperial		American
	1 banana, unpeeled	
	½ small onion, chopped	
	1 green chilli, de-seeded and finely chopped	
2 × 5ml spoons/ 2 teaspoons	cider vinegar	2 teaspoons
5 × 15ml spoons/ 5 tablespoons	yoghurt	6 tablespoons
	salt, freshly ground pepper	

Cook the banana in boiling water until soft, then cool. Peel, mash and mix with the onion and chilli. Add the vinegar and yoghurt, then season to taste.

AND TO FINISH . . .

EASTERN APPLES

Metric/imperial		American
450g/1 lb	cooking apples, peeled and sliced	1 lb
	6 glacé (candied) cherries, chopped	
1 × 15ml spoon/ 1 tablespoon	flaked (slivered) almonds	1 tablespoon
1 × 15ml spoon/ 1 tablespoon	raisins	1 tablespoon
2 × 15ml spoons/ 2 tablespoons	honey	3 tablespoons
2 × 5ml spoons/ 2 teaspoons	candied peel	2 teaspoons
1 × 2.5ml spoon/ ½ teaspoon	cinnamon	½ teaspoon

Put the apples in a pan with a little water, and cook for 5–8 minutes until soft. Mash with a fork, then fold in the other ingredients, and serve topped with yoghurt.

APPLE, DATE AND OATMEAL PIE

Metric/imperial		American
100g/4 oz	margarine	½ cup
100g/4 oz	porridge oats	generous 1 cup
100g/4 oz	wholemeal (wholewheat) flour	1 cup
100g/4 oz	soft brown sugar	½ cup
450g/1 lb	cooking apples, sliced	1 lb
	rind and juice of 1 lemon	
50g/2 oz	stoned (pitted) dates	⅓ cup

Rub (cut in) the margarine into the oats and flour until crumbly. Mix with the sugar, then bind with a little water. Divide into two pieces, and press one piece into a 20cm/8 inch flan tin (pie pan).

Put the apples in a pan with the lemon rind and juice and a little water, and cook until the apples are soft.

Fill the pastry case (pie shell) with the stewed apples, and arrange the dates on top. Roll out the second piece of the pastry, and place it on top of the pie. Bake in a fairly hot oven, 200°C/400°F/Gas 6, for 1 hour. Serve hot or cold with yoghurt.

Note The pastry is very crumbly, and it may be necessary to roll it into two halves, joining the pastry with a little water across the centre.

Rhubarb and Walnut Ginger Crumble

Metric/imperial		American
450g/1 lb	rhubarb, chopped	1 lb
2 × 15ml spoons/ 2 tablespoons	Barbados (raw cane) sugar **or** honey	3 tablespoons
	juice of 1 lemon	
65g/2½ oz	butter **or** margarine	5 tablespoons
100g/4 oz	wholemeal (wholewheat) flour, sifted	1 cup
25g/1 oz	chopped walnuts	¼ cup
50g/2 oz	light Muscovado (raw cane) sugar	¼ cup
	a little ground ginger	
25g/1 oz	raisins	2 tablespoons

Put the rhubarb in a pan with the sugar or honey, the lemon juice and enough water to cover about two-thirds of the rhubarb, and cook until the rhubarb is soft.

Meanwhile, rub (cut in) the fat into the flour, and mix with the nuts, Muscovado (raw cane) sugar and the ginger.

Put the rhubarb in a large oval ovenproof dish, mix with the raisins, and sprinkle with the crumble mixture, pressing down lightly. Bake in a moderate oven, 180°C/350°F/Gas 4, for about 40–45 minutes until golden-brown.

Orange Nut Crumble

Metric/imperial		American
450g/1 lb	prepared fruit (apples, plums or gooseberries)	1 lb
50g/2 oz	honey	3 tablespoons
75g/3 oz	butter **or** margarine	6 tablespoons
100g/4 oz	wholemeal (wholewheat) flour, sifted	1 cup
50g/2 oz	ground almonds, peanuts **or** hazel-nuts (filberts)	½ cup
75g/3 oz	Barbados (raw cane) sugar	6 tablespoons
	juice and grated rind of 1 orange	

Put the fruit in a pan with the honey and a little water, and cook until soft.

Meanwhile, rub (cut in) the fat into the flour and nuts until the mixture is crumbly, then add the sugar and orange rind.

Put the fruit into a greased 600ml/1 pint 2½ US cup pie dish, pour over the orange juice, then sprinkle with the crumble mixture, and press down lightly. Bake in a fairly hot oven, 190°C/375°F/Gas 5, for about 30 minutes.

Serve with yoghurt.

Note This dish can be started in a hot oven, 220°C/425°F/Gas 7, then turned down to fairly hot, 190°C/375°F/Gas 5, after about 10–15 minutes.

Pear and Ginger Crumble Pudding

Metric/imperial		American
50g/2 oz	butter **or** margarine	4 tablespoons
100g/4 oz	muesli (granola)	1 cup
50g/2 oz	Barbados (raw cane) sugar	$\frac{1}{4}$ cup
675g/1$\frac{1}{2}$ lb	pears, peeled, cored and sliced	1$\frac{1}{2}$ lb
	1 piece of stem ginger, chopped with a little ginger syrup	
6 × 15ml spoons/ 6 tablespoons	water	7 tablespoons

Melt the butter in a pan and mix in the muesli (granola) and sugar. Place half the pears and the ginger in an ovenproof dish, and cover with half the muesli (granola) mixture. Repeat these two layers, then pour on the water and a little ginger syrup. Bake in a moderate oven, 180°C/350°F/Gas 4, for 1 hour. Serve hot or cold with yoghurt.

Hazelnut Soufflé

Metric/imperial		American
	milk	
25g/1 oz	butter **or** margarine	2 tablespoons
	a pinch of salt	
50g/2 oz	sugar	$\frac{1}{4}$ cup
65g/2$\frac{1}{2}$ oz	wholemeal (wholewheat) flour, sifted	$\frac{1}{2}$ cup + 2 tablespoons
	4 eggs, separated	
100g/4 oz	ground roasted hazelnuts (filberts)	1 cup

Heat together the milk, butter, salt and sugar in a pan. Add the flour gradually, then stir until the mixture forms a smooth paste which comes away easily from the sides of the pan. Leave to cool.

Beat together the yolks and ground hazelnuts (filberts), and add to the cooled sauce mixture. Whisk the whites until stiff peaks form, then fold into the mixture. Pour into a greased 900ml/1$\frac{1}{2}$ pint/3$\frac{3}{4}$ US cup soufflé dish, and bake in a moderate oven, 180°C/350°F/Gas 4, for 1 hour. Serve immediately.

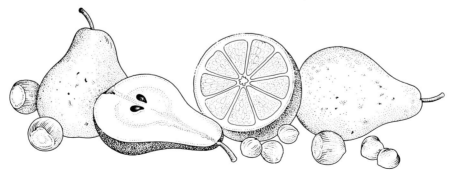

ADUKI PIE

Metric/imperial		American
50g/2 oz	margarine **or** butter	4 tablespoons
100g/4 oz	wholemeal (wholewheat) flour, sifted	1 cup
	a pinch of salt	
75g/3 oz	cooked Aduki beans	generous $\frac{1}{2}$ cup
50g/2 oz	raisins	$\frac{1}{3}$ cup
450g/1 lb	cooking apples, peeled, cored and sliced	1 lb
	juice of 1 lemon	
2 × 15ml spoons/ 2 tablespoons	honey	3 tablespoons
	ground cinnamon	
	apricot jam, melted	

Rub (cut in) the fat into the flour and salt, and bind with water. Roll out on a lightly floured surface, and use to line a 17.5cm/7 inch flan tin (pie pan). Cover with the beans and raisins, then follow with the apples. Pour over the lemon juice and honey, and sprinkle with cinnamon. Brush with melted apricot jam. Bake in a fairly hot oven, 200°C/400°F/Gas 6, for 45–50 minutes until lightly browned.

ORANGE DELIGHT

Metric/imperial		American
	4 oranges	
2 × 15ml spoons/ 2 tablespoons	wheatgerm	3 tablespoons
	yoghurt	
2 × 15ml spoons/ 2 tablespoons	desiccated (shredded) coconut	3 tablespoons

DECORATION
maraschino
cherries

Grate the rind of two oranges and mix with the wheatgerm. Peel and segment all the oranges, and dip the segments in the yoghurt. Roll half in the wheatgerm and orange rind and the rest in the coconut. Arrange on a serving plate, and decorate with maraschino cherries.

Aduki Pie **and** *Orange Delight*

PLUM CHEESECAKE

Metric/imperial		American
	9 unsweetened wheatmeal biscuits (wholewheat cookies), crushed	
75g/3 oz	margarine **or** butter, melted	6 tablespoons
225g/8 oz	fresh plums, stoned (pitted)	½ lb
3 × 15ml spoons/ 3 tablespoons	clear honey	4 tablespoons
225g/8 oz	quark (low-fat cheese)	1 cup
150ml/¼ pint	soured cream	⅔ cup
	2 eggs, separated	
	rind and juice of 1 lemon	
150ml/¼ pint	yoghurt	⅔ cup

Mix together the biscuits with one-third of the fat, and press into the base of a 22.5cm/9 inch loose-bottomed cake tin (spring-form pan). Cover with the plums.

Cream together the remaining fat with 2 × 15ml spoons/2 tablespoons/3 US tablespoons honey until light and fluffy, then gradually beat in the quark, soured cream and the yolks. Add a little lemon juice and some grated lemon rind. Whisk the whites until stiff, then fold them in.

Pour the cheese mixture into the cake tin (pan), and bake in a moderate oven, 180°C/350°F/Gas 4, for 1 hour until set and golden-brown.

Beat together the yoghurt and remaining honey with a little more lemon juice, and pour this over the top of the cheesecake. Smooth with a palette knife (metal spatula). Bake in a cool oven, 150°C/300°F/Gas 2, for a further 15 minutes until set.

COFFEE CHEESECAKE MOUSSE

Metric/imperial		American
	9 unsweetened wholemeal biscuits (wholewheat cookies), crushed	
25g/1 oz	sugar	2 tablespoons
40g/1½ oz	butter **or** margarine, melted	3 tablespoons
2 × 15ml spoons/ 2 tablespoons	honey	3 tablespoons
225g/8 oz	cream cheese	1 cup
	2 eggs, separated	
150ml/¼ pint	yoghurt	⅔ cup
2 × 5ml spoons/ 2 teaspoons	gelozone (vegetarian setting agent)	2 teaspoons
65ml/2½ fl oz	water	6 tablespoons
1 × 15ml spoon/ 1 tablespoon	instant coffee granules	1 tablespoon

Mix together the crushed biscuits (cookies) with the sugar and melted butter. Press into a 17.5cm/7 inch cake tin (pan), and bake in a very cool oven, 140°C/275°F/Gas 1, for 8–10 minutes. Leave to cool.

Meanwhile, mix the honey and cream cheese until smooth, then add the yolks and yoghurt. Blend the gelozone (setting agent) with the water and coffee granules, then heat to boiling point, and simmer for 2–3 minutes. Leave to cool, then mix with the cheese and egg. Whisk the whites until stiff, then fold into the cheese mixture. Pour this into the biscuit base, then chill until firm.

Apricot Meringue Gâteau

Metric/imperial		American
100g/4 oz	dried apricots	$\frac{2}{3}$ cup
	2 egg whites	
100g/4 oz	Muscovado (raw cane) sugar	$\frac{1}{2}$ cup
50g/2 oz	ground hazelnuts (filberts)	$\frac{1}{2}$ cup
	a pinch of bicarbonate of soda (baking soda)	
	vanilla essence (extract)	
1 × 15ml spoon/ 1 tablespoon	honey	1 tablespoon
150ml/$\frac{1}{4}$ pint	water	$\frac{2}{3}$ cup
50g/2 oz	quark (low fat soft cheese)	$\frac{1}{4}$ cup
65ml/$2\frac{1}{2}$ fl oz	double (heavy) cream	6 tablespoons
1 × 15ml spoon/ 1 tablespoon	chopped nuts	1 tablespoon

Soak the apricots overnight in enough water to cover. Whisk the egg whites until very stiff, then gradually whisk in half the sugar. Fold in the rest of the sugar with the nuts, soda and vanilla essence (extract). Spread the meringue into two thin equal-sized rounds on rice paper on a baking sheet. Bake in a very cool oven, 120°C/240°F/Gas $\frac{1}{2}$, for about $2\frac{1}{2}$ hours until dried out. Leave to cool on a wire rack.

Meanwhile, drain the apricots, then simmer with the honey and the 150ml/$\frac{1}{4}$ pint/$\frac{2}{3}$ US cup water for 30 minutes until soft. Pass through a sieve or process in a blender or food processor, then leave to cool. Mix together the quark and cream, then whip together until thick.

Place a layer of meringue on a serving dish, spread with the apricot purée, and follow with a layer of whipped cream. Top with the second meringue, and sprinkle with chopped nuts.

Citrus Melon

Metric/imperial		American
	1 small honeydew melon, halved and flesh chopped	
	chopped segments of 1 grapefruit	
	chopped segments of 2 oranges	
50g/2 oz	roasted peanuts, chopped	$\frac{1}{2}$ cup
25g/1 oz	light Muscovado (raw cane) sugar	2 tablespoons
$\frac{1}{2}$ × 2.5ml spoon/ $\frac{1}{4}$ teaspoon	ground cinnamon	$\frac{1}{4}$ teaspoon

Mix the chopped melon with the grapefruit and oranges. Pile into the melon shell, and sprinkle with the peanuts, sugar and cinnamon.

APRICOTS IN GINGER

Metric/imperial		American
225g/8 oz	dried apricots	1⅓ cups
100ml/4 fl oz	ginger wine	½ cup
150ml/¼ pint	white wine	⅔ cup

Soak the apricots overnight in half the ginger wine, all the white wine and enough water to cover.

Pour the soaked apricots and their liquid into a large pan, then heat to boiling point. Simmer for 20–30 minutes until the apricots are cooked but not falling apart. Leave to cool, then transfer to a glass serving dish. Top with the remaining ginger wine, and serve with yoghurt.

PEARS IN ORANGE JUICE

Metric/imperial		American
1 × 5ml spoon/ 1 teaspoon	honey	1 teaspoon
	juice of 2 oranges	
	2 large, ripe pears, peeled, cored and halved	
1 × 15ml spoon/ 1 tablespoon	nuts, chopped	1 tablespoon

Mix the honey with the orange juice, then pour this over the halved pears. Chill until ready to serve, then sprinkle with the chopped nuts.

BANANA NUT DESSERT

Metric/imperial		American
	4 bananas, sliced	
150ml/¼ pint	yoghurt	⅔ cup
2 × 5ml spoons/ 2 teaspoons	flaked (slivered) almonds	2 teaspoons
2 × 5ml spoons/ 2 teaspoons	hazelnuts (filberts), chopped	2 teaspoons
2 × 5ml spoons/ 2 teaspoons	honey	2 teaspoons

Arrange the sliced bananas on a large serving plate. Mix the yoghurt with the rest of the ingredients, then pour this over the bananas. Chill until ready to serve.

A Choice Of Menu

Quick Everyday Menu

Shropska (page 16)

Pasta with Peanut Sauce (page 44)

Eastern Apples (page 69)

Weekend Family Meal

Stuffed Onions with Soya
and Rosemary (page 22)

Fennel Bean Pot (page 36)
with Spinach Mountain (page 58)

Citrus Melon (page 75)
or Orange Nut Crumble (page 70)

ENTERTAINING FRIENDS TO DINNER

Green Pea Soufflé (page 19)

African Curried Vegetables (page 40)
with Jollof Rice (page 60)
and Aubergine Corn (page 57)

Plum Cheesecake (page 74)

CELEBRATION OR SPECIAL ANNIVERSARY DINNER

Artichokes with Richelieu Sauce (page 18)

Apple and Celery Soup (page 31)

Cardamon Cheese Pie (page 34)
with Potato and Mushroom Celeste (page 39)
and Mexican Baked Spinach (page 43)

Hazelnut Soufflé (page 71)

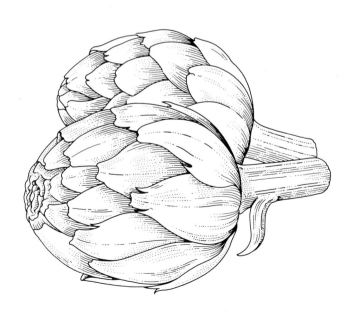

INDEX OF RECIPES